Lillian C. Masterman

The Common Sense Cook Book

Lillian C. Masterman

The Common Sense Cook Book

ISBN/EAN: 9783744788694

Printed in Europe, USA, Canada, Australia, Japan

Cover: Foto ©Lupo / pixelio.de

More available books at **www.hansebooks.com**

THE
COMMON SENSE
COOK BOOK.

A VOLUME OF PRACTICAL RECIPES, GIVING THOSE MINUTE DIRECTIONS, WITHOUT WHICH SUCCESS IN PREPARING DISHES IS FOR MANY UNATTAINABLE.

BY LILLIAN C. MASTERMAN.

PRESENTED WITH COMPLIMENTS
OF

THE WEINHOLD DRUG CO.

THREE STORES:

WEST HOTEL, HENNEPIN AVE., COR FIFTH ST.
NICOLLET AVE., AND GRANT ST.
FOURTH AVE. S. AND FRANKLIN AVE.

MINNEAPOLIS.

MINNEAPOLIS, 1894:
THE SWINBURNE PRINTING COMPANY,
ENGRAVERS AND PRINTERS.

Entered According to Act of Congress, in the Year 1894, by
LILLIAN C. MASTERMAN,
in the Office of the Librarian of Congress, at Washington, D. C.

INTRODUCTION.

To the Ladies of Minneapolis, Greeting:

In presenting to you the Common Sense Cook Book, we feel that we are offering something that will be appreciated. This work contains one thousand recipes of known and tried merit. It has been compiled in a thorough and systematic manner and we feel sure you will find in it a great deal of new and valuable information. We have been to an enormous expense, and have had a vast amount of work to do in getting this ready for your perusal.

Kindly remember us when concocting some delicious dish from our book for your better halves, family or friends, and if you or they are not already our customers, we should be pleased to have you become so.

Your friends,

THE WEINHOLD DRUG CO.

COTOSUET

BREAD.

NO PART of home cookery requires as much skill as bread making. The art of making good bread can only be attained by patient care and watchfulness. It is not necessarily a difficult task; yet I will venture to say that there are a large proportion of young American housekeepers who can make a good cake and prepare a delicious dessert, that cannot make a good loaf of bread.

Bread making should be one of the first lessons taught. What is more conducive to conjugal quarrels than heavy, sour bread? No article of food is as essential as good bread. With good bread in the house no one need ever go hungry. No meal, no matter how much is prepared for it, is complete without it. Good wheat flour is the basis of good bread. The best flour is not of a pure white color, but has a creamy, yellowish white tinge. Never buy flour that looks blue white. If it feels clammy or forms in lumps it is not of the best. Good flour holds together in a mass and adheres to the hand; and when squeezed retains the imprint of the fingers, and even the lines of the skin, longer than poor flour when made into dough. If good it will be elastic and take up a large quantity of water, and stay in shape longer. Poor flour will flatten and spread. Never use flour without sifting. Keep it in a dry, cool place and not a great quantity of any kind on hand, as it is very apt to become musty. There are two ways of making bread by fermentation, and bread made without fermentation. By fermentation we mean the setting free of carbonic gas, which spreads rapidly through the whole mass of dough, and causes it to rise by the rapid multiplication of new air cells upon those already formed. Yeast causes the process of fermentation. The cells in the yeast plant are very small and when the temperature is such as to cause them to grow rapidly, and coming in contact with any substance like dough, they increase so rapidly that the whole mixture is filled with them. Sour milk and soda cause the same process to take place. Baking powders cause the dough to rise quickly. The importance of having good yeast is readily seen. What is yeast? Yeast is a plant or germ of the lowest order of vegetable growth. It contains numberless minute oval cells; each cell contains a sap. They multiply by millions very rapidly. These are propagated in anything where they find congenial food. Grape juice in two hours' standing in a warm place will give off a froth of yeast cells. Bread made with yeast is much more porous, lighter, and pleasanter to the taste, and much more easily digested. Good bread should be of a light spongy texture, and to get this we allow the bread, under the influence of the yeast, to expand as much as possible without becoming sour. Unfermented bread is made without yeast. The principle is the same, being the liberation of gas. The usual method is by some gas generating compound, as the union of soda and sour milk. When chemicals used are in such a proportion that they are neutralized and leave only Rochelle salt, this bread is harmless but not so palatable and digestable as yeast bread. The three essential elements of good bread are good yeast, the best flour and an even temperature. There are three kinds of yeast, any of them are good; dry, compressed and liquid. Compressed yeast is only good when it can be obtained fresh. Potato yeast is the best, as bread made from it does not dry up so quickly and is sweeter and more nutritious.

First set your sponge. This is made from warm water or milk, yeast and flour. If you do not use potato yeast, use the water in which the potatoes were cooked at dinner time, or add a few potatoes mashed and run through a sieve. In winter make the water or milk quite warm. In summer have it lukewarm. Do not sponge too early in the evening, as the sponge is apt to stand too long before it is mixed and kneaded. If compressed yeast is used (this is one of the most rapid forms of fermentation), sponge before breakfast. Use about one cup of liquid yeast to one quart of wetting. If compressed yeast is used, use one-half a cake to the same quantity. If milk is used, scald to prevent its souring. In winter warm the flour and all dishes used. Keep the temperature even; about 75 degrees should be kept up during the entire process. Mix as soon as the sponge has risen to the proper point. You can tell this by its light, puffy appearance, the middle standing higher than the sides. If it looks fallen in the middle, it has stood too long. Knead well, and thoroughly for at least twenty minutes. This is very important. Knead until the mass of dough feels light, spongy and elastic under the hand. To knead the bread well requires strength and patience. A little sugar is necessary to bread, and if the bread is made of water, a little shortening of some kind. A word about the baking. This is one of the important parts of the whole process. The excellence of the bread is greatly dependent upon the perfection of the cells produced by the action of heat upon carbonic acid gas. The oven should be hot when the bread is put in. The heat should be of sufficient strength to last through the time of baking (which is always about one hour for an ordinary loaf of bread), without replenishing. It should increase at first, then diminish slowly toward the last. If the oven is too hot a hard brown crust will form and make the inside heavy. Do not remove before it is done or the mass will be heavy and raw inside. The dough should rise after fifteen minutes and brown slightly. Remove the loaves from the pans at once, as soon as the time is up, and place them where the air can circulate around freely. Turn the loaves out on a clean tea towel. Do not put away until cold, and then in a stone jar or a tin box. Keep the jar well covered to prevent the bread from drying.

Potato Yeast

Have three quarts of water boiling rapidly. Pare three raw potatoes, and let them soak awhile in cold water. Mix one-fourth of a cup of flour with one-fourth of a cup of sugar and one tablespoon of salt. Grate the potatoes, and add them to the flour, sugar and salt. Pour the boiling water on them. Pour part of it on the grater. Add water enough to make the yeast the consistency of thin starch. If this does not thicken cook awhile. Strain and cool. When lukewarm add one cup of yeast. Put in a warm place until the top is covered with bubbles. Beat it well. Cover tighly, and keep in a cool place. Add a little ginger; it improves it, and helps to keep the yeast.

Bread Sponge.

Take three potatoes, boiled, and mashed while hot, and dissolved in one quart of warm water, or one quart of potato water. Into this stir three cups of flour, and six tablespoons of good yeast. Beat to a smooth batter. Set over night. In the morning add a tablespoon of white sugar, a large tablespoon of white lard or butter. Knead well for twenty minutes, and set to rise. Knead down once more, and when light mold into loaves, and let it rise again very light. In place of liquid yeast use one-half a cake of compressed yeast or dry yeast.

Hop Yeast.

Steep half a cup of loose hops in one quart of boiling water five minutes. Mix one cup of flour, one-fourth of a cup of sugar, and one tablespoon of salt. Strain the hops and pour the liquor boiling on the flour. Boil a minute. Add a cup of yeast when cool, and put in a warm place to ferment.

MAY—Where shall I hang the mistletoe bough this year?
Jack—On your nose would about catch me.—Truth.

Log Cabin Maple Syrup.

Milk Bread.

Take one pint of milk, scalded and cooled. Put in a bowl, and add one tablespoon of butter, on tablespoon of sugar, one teaspoonful of salt. When lukewarm add one-half a cup of liquid yeast or a small half a cake of compressed yeast, and six cups of flour. Let it rise. When light knead until very smooth and elastic. Let it rise again, and when light mold into loaves. When light bake in a steady oven an hour. The time of course depends on the size of the loaves.

Rye Bread.

Pour one pint of scalded milk on one tablespoonful each of butter and sugar, and one teaspoonful of salt; when lukewarm add half a cup of yeast. Stir in three cups of rye flour or rye meal. Beat well, let it rise over night; in the morning add two cups of flour, and knead half a hour. Let it rise again, and mold into loaves and put to rise again; let it rise the last time very light.

Raised Brown Bread.

Put one pint of cornmeal in a bowl and scald it with boiling water enough to wet it. Let it stand awhile, then add cold water enough to make a soft batter. Now add half a cup of yeast, one-half a cup of molasses, one-half a teaspoon of salt, and one saltspoon of soda, one pint of rye meal. Beat thoroughly and let the mixture rise over night; in the morning stir it down and put it in a well greased tin; let it rise again. Bake in a slow oven two hours.

Steamed Brown Bread.

One egg, one cup of molasses, four cups of sour milk, one tablespoon of shortning, two teaspoonfuls of soda. Beat well together and add two cups of flour, and four cups of cornmeal; steam four hours, and bake fifteen minutes in a quick oven. Serve hot with baked beans.

Graham Bread.

Take one pint of good potato sponge, add one pint lukewarm water, one cup of brown sugar, teaspoon of salt; add Graham flour enough to make a stiff batter; put in baking tins and let the mixture rise again. Bake in a slow oven, and when done wrap in a towel and let it steam.

Eastern Brown Bread.

One cup of white cornmeal, one cup of rye flour, one cup of Graham flour, one teaspoon of salt, one teaspoon of soda, one-half cup of molasses, one pint of sour milk. Steam three hours.

☞ Caswell's Pectoral Balsam is a perfect cough cure.

Quick Corn Bread.

One pint of cornmeal, one pint of buttermilk, one egg, one teaspoon soda, one of salt; beat all together and bake in a dripping pan. A tablespoon of sugar improves it.

Bean Bread.

In the place of potatoes in bread reduce a pint of beans by boiling to a pulp. Extract the moisture and use the pulp in the sponge. Parsnips and sweet potatoes may be used in the same way.

Salt Rising Bread.

Take one pint of boiling water and a teaspoon of salt, when lukewarm stir in flour enough to make rather a stiff batter. Put it where it will be very warm overnight, in the morning set it in a kettle of very warm water, stir frequently, add half a teaspoon of soda dissolved in some warm water, stir well and leave to rise; when the dish is nearly full put a quantity of flour in the bread pan, put in a quart of water, quite warm, stir in some of the flour and then the rising batter, cover this with flour an inch thick and put in a warm place; when light make into loaves and put to rise again. Bake in a well heated oven nearly an hour.

Vienna Bread.

Take three pints of milk and water, teaspoon of salt, one cup of compressed yeast, two quarts of flour. Place the flour in a bread bowl, and put in the milk, water and salt. Make a thin batter. Add the yeast dissolved in a little lukewarm water. Beat well and cover the bowl and let it stand for three-quarters of an hour. At the end of that time mix in the rest of the flour. Let the dough stand for three hours until it is light and elastic. Cut into small pieces. Flatten these into squares, fold their corners to the center, pinch them down to hold them. Let them stand for ten minutes, turn them over again and let them stand a while longer. Put them in a hot oven. When they have risen, brush them with a sponge wet with milk, return to oven and finish baking.

Squash Bread.

One cup of squash stewed and sifted, one-half cup of sugar, two cups of scalded milk, teaspoon of salt, tablespoonful of butter, one-half cup of yeast or one-half cake of dry yeast. Mix squash, sugar and salt, add butter melted in hot milk, and when cool add yeast. Knead and let it rise very light. Mold into loaves and let it rise again. e

---

☞ Gentlemen will find Chap-O-Lene very beneficial applied immediately after shaving.

BREAKFAST AND TEA CAKES.

BISCUIT, muffins, griddle cakes, etc., are made with either sour or sweet milk. Soda must be used with something containing an acid, and is neutralized with sour milk. Soda is used in the proportion of one even teaspoon to a pint of thick sour milk, or buttermilk. Always pulverize your soda on the board with a knife before measuring, and sift into the flour. Some dissolve it in the milk, but in doing this some of the gas escapes in the effervescence. When sweet milk is used, use either soda and cream of tartar or baking powder. Use one level teaspoonful of soda to two of cream of tartar, and one quart of flour. It requires a little more than twice as much cream of tartar to neutralize the soda.

Use baking powder in the proportion of three rounding teaspoonfuls to one quart of flour. Always sift it thoroughly in the flour, use only the best cream of tartar. The pure article can be obtained best at a drug store. Soda biscuit must be made as quickly as possible. Baking powder biscuit must be mixed very soft, and handled as little as is necessary to get them in shape to cut out. Biscuit must be put in a hot oven, then cool the oven off gradually after they have risen until done a light brown. Molasses gives another acid, and is used with soda alone.

In making gems or muffins have your pans hot before pouring in the mixture. Waffles irons should be put on to heat when you commence to make your waffles. Grease on both sides with a cloth tied to the end of stick and used especially for this purpose. Lard or beef drippings are the best for greasing the irons. They require a longer time to bake than griddle cakes. Always sift your flour before measuring. In making rolls and raised biscuits, mold and set to rise two hours before baking.

Sour Cream Biscuit.

One quart of sifted flour, one even teaspoonful of salt, one even teaspoonful of soda, measured after it is pulverized, one pint of sour cream. If sweet cream is used, use with the soda two teaspoonfuls of cream of tartar. Sift soda and cream of tartar in the flour. Mix with the hands as little as possible.

Sour Milk Biscuit.

One quart of flour, one pint of sour milk, one teaspoon soda, sifted in the flour, one large tablespoon of butter, half a teaspoon of salt.

Soda Biscuit.

One quart flour, one teaspoon soda, two of cream of tartar, one of salt, one tablespoon of sugar; rub in a large tablespoon of lard or butter, wet with one pint of sweet milk. You can use instead of soda and cream of tartar three teaspoonfuls of baking powder. Leave out the sugar and by using more shortening, wet with the same quantity of water.

Baking Powder Biscuit.

One quart of flour, three heaping teaspoons of baking powder, a little salt, one pint of milk. The secret of success with these biscuit is mixing them very soft and baking in a quick, hot oven.

Milk Biscuit.

Two quarts of sifted flour, one pint milk boiled and cooled, one half cup of yeast, one teaspoonful of salt. Make hole in the flour and make a sponge of the milk and butter, let rise very light. Mold into small balls and let them rest again, and bake in a quick oven.

Muffins with Maple Sugar.

Take one pint of sour milk, or buttermilk, one teaspoon of soda, one quart of flour, tablespoon of shortening. Mix and roll out in a long sheet. Have butter warmed very soft, spread over the sheet of dough and cover with maple sugar. Roll up like roll jelly cake, cut off in slices. Put in a tin and bake in a quick oven. These are delicious for tea.

Velvet Biscuit.

One quart of milk, four eggs, one cup sugar, one-half cup butter, one yeast cake; roll thin and cut with cake cutter. Butter and let rise very light.

Muffins.

One cup of milk, one of flour, one teaspoon of sugar, two eggs, a little salt. Beat all till light and very smooth; pour in hot gem pans and bake twenty minutes.

Muffins. 2.

One teacup sweet milk, two eggs, two cups of flour, one heaping teaspoon of baking powder, a little salt, butter size of an egg. Bake in hot gem pans and cut immediately.

Buns.

Break an egg in a cup, fill with sweet milk, add one-fourth of a cup of butter, one-fourth cup sugar, one-half cup yeast. Flavor with either nutmeg or cinnamon; let rise until very light and mix in a few currants. Mold into very small balls, and after rising a second time glaze with a little molasses and milk. Bake twenty minutes, a delicate brown.

Parker House Rolls.

Rub one-half cup of butter into two quarts of sifted flour, add one pint of milk scalded and cooled, one-half cup yeast, a little salt, two tablespoons of white sugar. Make a hole in the flour, pour in milk, yeast and salt; let rise over night; in the morning knead and let stand until tea time. Mold and cut with cake cutter; put a little melted butter on one half and lap over the other half, let rise again and bake quickly.

Johnny Cake.

Piece of butter size of an egg, two tablespoons of sugar, cup and a half of sour milk, even teaspoon of soda, one egg, one-third cup of flour and small cup of meal. Bake in a long tin and cut in squares.

Johnny Cake. 2.

Two-thirds teaspoon of soda, three teaspoons of sugar, one teaspoon of cream of tartar, one egg, one cup of sweet milk, six tablespoons of Indian meal and three of flour. This makes a thin batter.

Sally Lunn.

One cup of scalded and cooled milk, one-half teaspoon of salt, one teaspoonful of sugar, one-fourth cup of yeast, one egg. Flour enough to make a drop batter; let them stand five or six hours and rise; then add one large tablespoon of butter. Bake in hot gem pans.

Graham Gems.

Two cups Graham flour, one tablespoon of sugar, two eggs, one cup of milk, one cup of water, teaspoonful of salt. Bake thirty minutes.

Gems, (without soda or Eggs.)

One cup of water, one cup of milk, one salt-spoon of salt, two and a half cups of Graham flour. Bake in very hot buttered gem pans.

Graham Gems.

One egg, two tablespoons of sugar, butter size of an egg, cup of sweet milk, two teaspoons of baking powder; Graham flour to make a thick batter. Mix baking powder with flour, melt butter, mix with sugar and lastly add milk and egg.

Graham Gems. 2.

One egg, butter size of an egg, three tablespoons of sugar, cup and a half of buttermilk or sour milk, one level teaspoon of soda; Graham flour to make a thick batter.

Gems.

One pint flour, one pint milk, one egg, a little salt. Bake twenty minutes in a hot oven.

Corn Gems.

Two cups cornmeal, one cup flour, two eggs, three teaspoons of baking powder, half a cup of butter, half a cup of sugar, a little salt; put in hot gem pans and bake twenty minutes.

Griddle Cakes.

One pint good sour milk or buttermilk, one teaspoon soda, two well beaten eggs, flour to make a soft batter. Beat yolks and whites separately.

Oat Meal Griddle Cakes.

To the above recipe add less flour and one cup of cooked oatmeal left from breakfast.

Bread Cakes.

Soak bread crumbs over night in a pint of sour milk, add two eggs, tablespoon of butter, teaspoon of soda and cornmeal to make them like griddle cakes. Some beat yolks and whites separately. It makes griddle cakes very light.

Buckwheat Cakes.

Take one quart of warm water, add five teacups of buckwheat flour and one of white flour, a little salt. Thin in the morning with one teacup of milk, half milk can be used with the water; use one-half yeast cake or one cup of good yeast. Let them rise over night, in the morning add one-fourth of a teaspoon of soda. What batter is left can be used a second time by adding more milk and water and half a teaspoon of soda.

Buckwheat Cakes. 2.

Pour one pint of boiling water on one cup of cornmeal and half a teaspoon of salt. Mix well and when lukewarm add one-half cup of white flour and one cup of buckwheat flour; one-half cup of yeast. Let them rise over night, in the morning beat down and add one-fourth a teaspoonful of soda.

☞ WE guarantee our work. If it is not entirely satisfactory send it back; don't use it up and then ask for a rebate, as you won't get it. We don't care to deal with cranks. The Swinburne Printing Company.

Cornmeal Griddle Cakes

One-half cup of flour, one cup of cornmeal, one pint of sour cream, teaspoon of soda.

Waffles.

One pint of flour, one teaspoonful of baking powder, one-half teaspoon of salt, two eggs, one and one-fourth cups sweet milk, one tablespoon of melted butter. Have your waffle irons hot. Brown on one side and turn.

Waffles. 2.

One pint of sweet milk, one-half cup of butter, three eggs, two teaspoons of baking powder, flour enough to make a soft batter. Beat whites and yolks of eggs separately.

Raised Waffles.

One quart of flour, one pint of sweet warm milk, two eggs, two tablespoons of melted butter, a little salt, half a teacupful of yeast, or one-half cake of any kind of yeast. Let them rise over night.

Pop Overs.

Two teacups of sweet milk, two teacups of sifted flour, butter size of a walnut, two eggs, one tablespoon of sugar, a little salt. Bake in hot gem pans and eat while hot. They are nice served with maple syrup or raspberry jam.

Corn Mush.

Take three pints of water, salt and let come to a boil; stir in meal, letting it sift through the fingers until it is as thick as can be stirred with the hand. Let it stand on top of stove in pan of water, and cook slowly for an hour.

To fry for breakfast add flour to the above mixture. Slice in thin slices, frying in hot lard, or dip in beaten eggs and then in cracker crumbs and fry in hot lard. Serve with maple syrup.

Toast.

Use bread two days old. Brown over quick fire. First warm each side of the bread, then put the first side to the fire and let it remain until it is a rich brown, then turn the other side to the fire. This extracts the moisture and makes the bread very digestable. Cut the slices uniform, about half an inch thick. Butter as soon as it is removed from the fire.

"THERE is a book with the title: 'How to Be Happy Though Married.' Doesn't fill the bill for old maids. They want a book that will tell them how to be happy though unmarried."

Milk Toast.

Toast the bread as given above; take one pint of milk, one tablespoon of cornstarch, one-half teaspoon of salt and a large lump of butter. Stir the cornstarch mixed with a little cold milk in the hot milk and let come to a boil. Put toast in a deep dish, and pour the cream over it. Let it stand in the oven a few minutes, and serve hot. Some add a well beaten egg the last thing to the cream. A good plan is to fry the flour in the butter.

French Toast.

Take two eggs, beaten light, add one cup of sweet milk; dip slices of dry bread in this mixture and fry on a well buttered griddle.

German Toast.

Chop fine nice tender beef, veal or chicken, season with butter, salt and pepper, a little sage or thyme if desired. Add enough water to make a thin mixture. Let boil five minutes and spread on slices of toast. Serve hot.

Tomato Toast.

Stew a quart of tomatoes, season with butter, salt and pepper, and sugar to taste, add a little minced onion if desired; strain and pour over large slices of buttered toast. Just before serving add a cup of cream; this makes it very nice. Serve hot and at once.

Welsh Rarebit.

One-fourth pound of rich cream cheese, one-fourth cup of cream or milk, one teaspoonful of mustard, one teaspoonful of salt, a little cayenne, one egg, piece of butter size of egg, four slices of toast. Grate the cheese, and put in the milk, add the rest of the ingredients. When the cheese has melted cook two minutes. Spread on the toast, and let stand in oven a few minutes, and serve immediately.

Welsh Rarebit. 2.

Allow a slice of toast for each person. Toast slightly and spread with butter. Take one cup or more grated cheese, large piece of butter, a little mustard, a pinch of salt, one egg, cayenne pepper a few grains, one cup of beer or enough to melt the cheese. Spread on the toast and serve immediately. Prepare as the recipe above says.   k

---

She Is Willing.

Mrs. Twynn—Don't you object to your husband playing poker so much?
Mrs. Triplett—Oh no! He nearly always wins.—Truth.

☞ THE cook will find something interesting on page 32.

Toasted Crackers.

Take large crackers. The salted zephyrettes are best. Spread with butter, pepper, salt and grated cheese; a little mustard if preferred. Brown a delicate color in a quick oven. These are nice to serve with salads, and are excellent with beer.

Sardines on Toast.

Mix the yolks of hard boiled eggs with an equal amount of sardines rubbed to a paste. Season with lemon juice, and salt and pepper and spread on buttered toast.

Codfish Toast.

Make a nice codfish cream, and pour over slices of buttered toast. Chipped beef in cream can be used the same way.

Raised Muffins.

Scald one pint of milk, add one tablespoon of butter, and stir until it is melted. When lukewarm add two teaspoonsfuls of sugar, two well beaten eggs, and one-quarter of a cup of yeast. Stir in the flour until thick enough to drop from a spoon. Let them stand, and rise over night. Lift out lightly in the morning, and drop by spoonfuls in hot muffin tins.

Crumpets.

Scald two cups of milk. Melt four tablespoonfuls of butter, add to the milk, and when lukewarm, add one teaspoonful of salt and three and one-half cups of flour. Add one-half a yeast cake dissolved in one-half cup of warm water. Beat well and let them stand in a warm place until very light, two hours. Bake in muffin rings on a hot griddle.

HAVE YOU ASTHMA OR BRONCHITIS?

Dr. R. Schiffmann, St. Paul, Minn., will mail a trial package of "Schiffmann's Asthma Cure" free to any sufferer. He advertises by giving it away. Never fails to give instant relief in worst cases and cures where others fail. Name this Cook Book and send address for a free trial package. Weinhold Drug Co. always keep a supply in stock.

Log Cabin Maple Syrup.

FEATHERSTONE—My ears were frost-bitten last winter, and I wouldn't be surprised if I had to wear ear-muffs this year.
Ringway—You'd better see about it right away.
Featherstone—Why? It isn't cold enough yet.
Ringway—Maybe not, old chap, but you will have to get them made to order.
—Truth.

☞ Caswell's Blood Cleaner will purify the blood.

☞ THE Swinburne Printing Company would like to see you when you have any use for printer's ink.

CAKE.

GATHER materials together, and have your table cleared of everything else. Put your butter where it will warm, but not melt. Eggs should be placed in the ice chest to cool so as to beat well. Always use the best butter for cake, as heat developes all its bad qualities. Have your sugar fine. First cream your butter and sugar, then add eggs beaten very light, then milk, and lastly flour and flavoring. Always sift the flour before measuring. If baking powder is used sift in the flour previously measured. If cream of tartar and soda are used, dissolve soda in the milk and sift cream tartar in the flour. Remember two things, sour milk makes light spongy cake, and soda should always be used with it. Sweet milk makes a firmer cake, and baking powder or cream tartar and soda should be used. Any light cake is improved by beating the whites to a stiff froth, and the yolks very light. The whites are stirred in the flour the last thing. In sponge cake the eggs must always be beaten separately and the flour sifted very light. Do not stir your mixture, but beat thoroughly, bringing the batter up from the bottom of the dish at each stroke. Use an earthen bowl in preference to tin. Use the same cup always for measuring. Those little tin ones with the halves and fourths marked are very handy. In fruit cake always seed your raisins by pouring boiling water on them. Cut your citron or candied fruit into small pieces. Always wash currants thoroughly and dry in a sieve. Brown your flour. Add fruit last thing well floured.

The baking of the cake is of as much importance as the mixing. Let your oven be hot when you put your cake in, then keep it at an even temperature. Do not shake oven or open too often, as an unequal temperature will cause it to fall. Layer cakes require a brisk fire; large cakes, a slow steady fire. In baking fruit cakes it is a good plan to put two or three thicknesses of well greased writing paper on the bottom of your pan. Molasses in dark cakes burns very quickly.

To test your cake to see if it is done use a splinter from a new broom, or a steel knitting needle. If nothing adheres to them, or if the cake, as we say, has stopped "singing," it is done. Grease tins always with lard or cottosuet. If almonds are used blanch by pour-

CHAP-O-LENE

Will positively cure all roughness of the skin.

Caswell's Pectoral Balsam

Is very highly recommended for Coughs, Colds and all Affections of the Throat, Chest and Lungs. It is guaranteed to give satisfaction.

Child's Cough Cure

Is prepared expressly for children and is not attended by the least danger, as is the case with cough remedies prepared for adults, the dose of which must be reduced when given to children.

Caswell's Beef, Wine and Iron

Is the best preparation of that universal and efficient Tonic.

CASWELL'S BLOOD CLANER

Will Purify your Blood.

These Preparations are Sold Exclusively ..by..

The Weinhold Drug Co.

LEADING PRESCRIPTION DRUGGISTS,

Minneapolis.

THREE STORES,

Fourth Avenue South and Franklin, Nicollet Avenue and Grant Street and West Hotel.

ing boiling water on them and when cold slip off skins and pound or chop. Cottosuet is an excellent substitute for butter for shortening cake, and is very much cheaper.

Delicate Cake.

Half teacup of butter, one of sugar, one and a half of flour, one-half cup of sweet milk, whites of four eggs, teaspoon of baking powder; flavor with lemon or vanilla.

Confectionery Cake.

Whites of five eggs, two cups of sugar, three-fourths cup of butter, two and a half cups of flour, one cup of sweet milk, two teaspoons of baking powder.

DARK PART.—Take one-half cup of white mixture, add one-half teacup of molasses, good one-half cup of flour, half a cup of raisins, one-half cup of currants, one-half teaspoon of soda, wineglass of brandy or two table-spoons of water, one-half teaspoon each of cinnamon, cloves and nutmeg; bake in three tins; use dark layer for center; put together with any kind of icing. Nuts or candied fruit chopped in it makes a very rich cake.

Spice Cake.

One pint of sugar, one pint of flour, one-half pint of milk, one cup of butter, four eggs, three teaspoons of baking powder, one teaspoon each of cinnamon, cloves and nutmeg. One teaspoon of soda, and two of cream tartar can be used in place of baking powder. Half of this recipe makes a good cake.

Cocoanut Cake.

One and a half cups of sugar, two tablespoons of butter, two eggs, two cups of flour mixed with two teaspoons baking powder, one cup sweet milk. Bake in three layers.

FILLING.—One cup of grated or desiccated cocoanut, one-half cup sweet milk, two-thirds of a cup of sugar. Boil till quite a jelly. Put any kind of icing on top and sprinkle with the dry cocoanut.

Chocolate Cream Cake.

One cup sugar, half teacup of butter, one and a half of flour, half cup sweet milk, whites of four eggs, heaping teaspoon baking powder. Bake in a long or square loaf. For the top take a cup and a half of granulated sugar, one-half cup milk, boil four minutes after it commences to boil, beat to a cream and spread while warm on top of cake. Shave off a small cup of Baker's chocolate, and melt on back of stove; spread over the cream and put away to harden.

Angels Food.

Whites of eleven eggs beaten to a stiff froth, one and a half cups sugar, one coffee cup flour, one teaspoon cream of tartar, one-half teaspoon vanilla. Sift flour several times before adding cream of tartar, this makes it very light; add pinch of salt and whites lastly in the flour. Bake in a slow oven about an hour.

Sponge Cake.

Three eggs, one and half cups granulated sugar, two of sifted flour, half cup cold water, two teaspoons cream of tartar and one of soda, grated rind and juice of one lemon. Bake in a dripping pan. Beat yolks and whites separately.

Sponge Cake. 2.

Yolks of three eggs, one cup granulated sugar, one tablespoon of lemon juice, one of cold water, one cup of sifted flour; add whites beaten stiff.

Sponge Cake. 3.

Six eggs, two teacups pulverized sugar; beat yolks and sugar to a cream, add one and half cups of flour with two small teaspoons of baking powder in it. Add whites beaten stiff till the top is covered with bubbles.

Sponge Cake. 4.

Ten eggs, two and a half cups of sugar, two and a half of flour, the juice and grated rind of one lemon. Beat yolks and sugar very light, add lemon, then the whites. Bake in a pan, the mixture to be about the depth of three inches.

Hickory Nut Cake.

One cup of granulated sugar, two-thirds cup sweet milk, one-half cup butter, two eggs, one cup chopped hickory nuts, two cups of flour, two teaspoons of baking powder.

Fig Cake.

One and a half cups of sugar, small half cup of butter, two eggs, one cup of sweet milk, two cups of flour, two teaspoons of baking powder. Bake in layers.

Filling for Fig Cake.

Take one-half pound of best figs, chop fine, one pint of water, one tablespoon of vinegar. Cook slowly till a thick jelly, add more water if necessary. Spread between layers and ice the top.

Child's Cough Cure is prepared especially for children.

Molasses Cake.

Two eggs, cup of molasses, one-half cup light brown sugar, one-half cup of butter, two thirds of a cup of sour milk or butter milk, small even teaspoon of soda, flour enough to make not a very stiff batter, one-half teaspoon each of cinnamon and cloves.

Ginger Cake.

Two cups of molasses, one cup melted butter, two teaspoons of soda disolved in one cup of hot water, two teaspoons of ginger, or one of nutmeg, flour enough to make a stiff batter. Always bake molasses or ginger cake in a very slow oven for molasses burns very quickly.

Ginger Drop Cakes.

Half cup sugar, cup of molasses, half cup butter, one teaspoon each of cinnamon, cloves and ginger. Two teaspoons of soda in a cup of boiling water, two and a half cups of flour, two well beaten eggs. Bake in gem tins, or drop in spoonfuls some distance apart in a well greased dripping pan.

Spanish Bun Cake.

Two teacups sugar, two teacups flour, one cup sweet milk, one-half cup butter, four eggs, one teaspoon each of cinnamon and cloves, one teaspoon soda, and two of cream tartar, or three teaspoons baking powder. Lastly add one half cup of chopped raisins or currants.

Common Fruit Cake.

One cup butter, two cups brown sugar, one cup molasses, one cup sour milk, four eggs, four cups flour, one pound of raisins, one half pound currants, one fourth pound of citron; candied lemon is also used, spice to taste, one teaspoon soda. This makes a very nice common fruit cake.

Wedding Cake.

One pound of butter, one pound of sugar, twelve eggs, one pound flour, two teaspoons each of cinnamon and mace, one teaspoon of nutmeg and allspice, one half teaspoon of cloves, two pounds of raisins, two pounds of currants, one pound of citron, one half pound of lemon peel, one pound of almonds, one wine glass brandy, one lemon. Use dark brown sugar, cream sugar and butter, add beaten yolks and beaten whites, then lemon juice, brandy, flour browned a little, and lastly fruit well dredged with flour. Blanch and chop almonds fine. This will make two cakes. Bake in a moderate oven three hours. p

---

☞ EVERY business man can profit if he will carefully follow the recipe on page 32.

COTOSUET

Made only by
SWIFT AND COMPANY.

COTOSUET is composed of the best cooking Cotton Seed Oil and Beef Suet, and mixes more thoroughly than Lard in pastry and cake.

COTOSUET contains no Hog Fat and is a pure and wholesome cooking material.

DIRECTIONS FOR USING COTOSUET.

COTOSUET is used exactly the same as lard in cooking. Use only one-half or two thirds the amount of COTOSUET that you would of lard. Always apply to the pan before heating. All cooking fats will have a burnt odor if put in a hot pan.
Try the following recipe for Doughnuts: 1 tablespoon COTOSUET, 1 cup Milk, 1 Cup Sugar, 2 Eggs, light tablespoon Baking Powder, 1 pinch Mace, 1 pinch Salt, Flour enough to make stiff dough, about 2 cups. Fry in COTOSUET.

RECOMMENDED BY MRS. MASTERMAN.

Orange Cake.

Two-thirds of a cup of butter, cup and a half of sugar, one cup milk, yolks of five eggs, two and a half small cups flour, two teaspoons baking powder. Bake in layers. Beat whites of three eggs stiff; pulverized sugar to consistency; juice and grated peal of one orange. Put white frosting on top and lay pieces of an orange in it.

Lemon Jelly Cake.

One cup and a half of sugar, one half cup butter, two eggs, one cup sweet milk, two cups of flour mixed with two teaspoons baking powder. Jelly—One cup sugar, two tablespoons butter, two eggs, juice of two lemons. Beat all together and boil in a double cooker till the consistency of jelly. Oranges can be used in place of lemons.

Cream Cakes.

One cup hot water, one-half teaspoon salt, one-half cup butter, one and a half cups flour, five eggs, beaten whites and yolks separately. Boil water, salt and butter, add flour slowly while boiling, stir for five minutes and when cool add eggs. Mix with hands and drop in tablespoon on a buttered baking pan some distance apart. When cool split and fill with cream made as follows: Cream—One pint milk, two tablespoons corn starch, three eggs well beaten, three-fourths cup sugar, one saltspoon salt, one teaspoon butter. Cook in double boiler five minutes, and when cool flavor with almond or vanilla. Fill with whipped cream.

Orange Cake. 2.

Two eggs, one cup sugar, one tablespoon melted butter, one-half cup milk, one and a half cups flour, two teaspoons baking powder, tablespoon orange juice and grated rind.

CREAM.—Grated rind and half the juice of an orange, one tablespoon lemon juice. Put this in a cup and fill with water, strain, and add one tablespoon corn starch, yolk of one egg, two tablespoons sugar, teaspoon butter. Boil till a jelly. Frost top and cover with pieces of orange.

Banana Cake.

One whole egg and yolks of two, one cup sugar, piece of butter size of an egg, one cup sweet milk, two and one-fourth cups flour, two teaspoons baking powder. Bake in two large sized jelly tins.

FILLING.—Beat whites of two eggs stiff with sugar, slice four bananas. Put frosting and bananas between layers and on top.

Roll Jelly Cake.

Three eggs, one cup sugar, one cup flour, one teaspoon cream of tartar, one-half teaspoon soda in flour. Bake slowly in a long tin and roll up while warm, wrapping in a cloth.

Bride's Cake.

Whites of twelve eggs, three cups sugar, one and one-half cups of butter, one cup sweet milk, one-half cup corn starch, two-thirds teaspoon soda, one and a half teaspoons cream tartar, flavor with vanilla; four cups of flour.

Caramel Cake.

One-half cup of butter, one teacup of sugar, one and a half teacups flour, one-half cup of sweet milk, whites of four eggs, one heaping teaspoon baking powder.

CARAMEL.—One and three-fourths cups of best brown sugar, one-half cup sweet milk, butter size of an egg, two teaspoons of vanilla, two and one-half bars of grated chocolate or one-fourth pound of Baker's chocolate.

Fig Cake or Cocoanut.

One cup of butter, two cups of sugar, three and a half cups of flour, one cup sweet milk, whites of five eggs, one heaping teaspoon baking powder. One cup of desiccated cocoanut, or one-half pound of figs cut up fine and well floured, stirred in the batter makes a very rich cake. Bake in a loaf and ice the top.

Raised Cake.

Two cups very light dough, half cup of butter, cup and a half of sugar, four tablespoons of sour milk or buttermilk, half teaspoon soda, one teaspoon of cinnamon and cloves, half a nutmeg, cup of chopped raisins well floured; stir all together well, place where it is warm and let rise for half or three-quarters of an hour.

White Fruit Cake.

One cup of butter, two cups of sugar, one cup of sweet milk, whites of four eggs, two cups and a half of flour, two teaspoons baking powder, one-fourth pound of citron, half a pound of chopped almonds, one pound of seeded raisins and one-half cup of desiccated cocoanut if desired; chop fruit all fine, flour, and stir in the last thing. This will make two loaves and should be baked in a moderate oven. r

☞ Caswell's Pectoral Balsam cures all coughs, colds and affections of the throat, chest and lungs.

"THE oculist and the dentist are always ready to furnish an eye for an eye and a tooth for a tooth."

Coffee Cake.

One cup of brown sugar, one-half cup of molasses, one-half cup of butter, two eggs, one half cup of strong coffee, one small teaspoon soda, one half teaspoon each of cloves, cinnamon and mace, one cup of raisins, one-half cup of currants, two cups of flour.

Chocolate Cake.

One cup butter, two of sugar, one of sweet milk, five eggs, leave out whites of two, three and a half of flour, small cups, one teaspoon cream tartar, half teaspoon soda or one and a half of baking powder. Bake in layers.

ICING.—The whites of two eggs, cup and a half of sugar, six tablespoons of grated chocolate, one teaspoon of vanilla. Put the chocolate, sugar and two tablespoons of water in a sucepan, stir until smooth and glossy over a hot fire, beat whites to a stiff froth; beat all together and spread between layers, and on top.

Walnut Cake.

One cup of sugar, half a cup of butter, half a cup of milk, two eggs, two cups of flour, one large cup of chopped raisins, and one cup of English walnuts, one teaspoon cream tartar, one-half teaspoon of soda, or two teaspoons baking powder. Bake in a loaf and ice, putting halves of the nuts on top.

Pork Cake.

One half pound of fat pork chopped fine, pour over it one cup of boiling water, add two cups of sugar, one-half cup of molasses, two eggs, four small cups of flour, one even teaspoon of soda, one teaspoon each of cinnamon, cloves and nutmeg. Bake in a slow oven. Add a pound of chopped raisins, and one-fourth pound of citron if desired.

Ice Cream Cake.

Make a good sponge cake, bake in layers, and let it get perfectly old. Take a pint of sweet cream, sweeten, whip, and flavor with vanilla; chop a pound of almonds and stir in the cream. This makes a delicious cake. The almonds can be left out.

Jelly Cake.

Half cup butter, two of sugar, one of sour cream, three of flour, three eggs, half teaspoon of soda. Bake in layers and spread with jelly.

☞ THE housekeeper should not fail to study page 32.

THE man who is proud of his old family, might snub its founders as upstarts if he had the chance.—Puck.

THE WEINHOLD DRUG CO.

Chew Beeman's Pepsin Gum.

A Delicious Remedy for Indigestion, and the Perfection of Chewing Gums.

BEWARE OF IMITATIONS.

ORIGINATED AND MANUFACTURED BY THE

Beeman Chemical Company,

CLEVELAND, OHIO.

Neapolitan Cake.

BLACK PART.—One cup brown sugar, two eggs, half cup butter, half cup molasses, half cup strong coffee, two and a half cups flour, one cup raisins, one-half cup currants, teaspoon soda, teaspoon each of cloves, cinnamon and mace.

WHITE PART.—Two cups white sugar, half cup butter, one of milk, two and a quarter of flour, one of corn starch, whites of four eggs, teaspoon of cream of tartar. Bake in layers and put all together with icing made of the whites of two eggs.

Huckleberry Cake.

One cup butter, two of sugar, three cups of flour, five eggs, one cup sweet milk, one teaspoon of soda, one teaspoon each of cinnamon and nutmeg, one quart of berries dredged with flour. Stir in carefully and bake in a loaf. Ice the top.

Poor Man's Cake.

Three cups bread dough, two cups sugar, one of butter, two eggs. Mix well; spice to taste and put in currants and raisins if preferred. Let rise and bake in a brisk oven. Do not use any flour.

Zephyr Cake.

Wash the salt out of three-quarters of a pound of butter, add a quarter of a pound powdered sugar, and three eggs, teaspoon rose water and sifted flour to make a thin batter. Stir until batter is so light that it will break when it falls against the side of the crock used in mixing. Bake in patty tins.

Maple Sugar Cake.

Three eggs, one cup sugar, two tablespoons sweet milk, one heaping cup of flour with two teaspoons of baking powder mixed in it.

FILLING.—Boil one cup of maple sugar to wax, beat white of one egg to stiff froth, pour sugar on it and beat quickly; spread between layers.

Excellent Spice Cake.

This is a delicious cake when made right. Take one egg, two-thirds of a cup of sugar, the same quantity of molasses and butter, cup of milk, two cupfulls and a half of flour, one teaspoon of soda, one level teaspoon of cream tarter, one tablespoon of vinegar or lemon juice, and one tablespoon of mixed spice. Beat egg well, add molasses, sugar, spice, butter, lastly add lemon juice. Bake in a shallow pan twenty minutes. t

The Weinhold Drug Co.

ARE THE LARGEST

Retail Druggists

IN MINNEAPOLIS.

THEY HAVE THREE STORES, LOCATED AS FOLLOWS:

**Fourth Ave. So. and Franklin,
Nicollet Ave. and Grant St.,
and at the West Hotel.**
(Fifth St. and Hennepin.)

The Prescription Departments

of all these stores are very complete in every way. The purest and best Drugs and Chemicals are always on hand and competent druggists in attendance.

A Very Nice Line of Druggist Sundries

can always be found comprising Brushes of all kinds, Combs, Sponges, Chamois Skins, Toilet Articles, Soaps, Etc.

Their Line of Perfumes

both bulk and in bottles is the best, both in quality and variety, to be found in the Northwest.

FAMILY TRADE is given especial attention and prescriptions, packages, etc., will always be cheerfully delivered. An inspection of their stores will convince you that they are all that is claimed for them.

Soliciting your patronage, we remain your friends,

THE WEINHOLD DRUG CO.

Whipped Cream Cake.

One egg, one cup sugar, one cup flour, half cup sweet milk, half teaspoon soda, teaspoon cream tartar, two tablespoons of butter. Bake in two layers. Take one cup of thick sweet cream, and beat till thick; sweeten and flavor with vanilla or lemon, and spread between layers and on top. This served with sliced oranges makes a delicious dessert, or put sliced bananas between the layers in the cream.

Cocoanut and Raisin Cream.

One cup of butter, one and a half cups sugar, three eggs beaten separately, one teaspoonful lemon or vanilla, saltspoon of mace, one-half cup milk, three cups flour, teaspoonful cream tartar, one half teaspoonful soda. Bake in three layers.

FILLING.—One cup of raisins stoned and chopped, half cup grated cocoanut. Stir these in a boiled frosting made of the white of one egg, and small teacup of granulated sugar. (See Icings.)

Corn Starch Cake.

One half cup butter, one and a half cups sugar, one-half cup milk, one-half teaspoon of almond flavoring, one-half cup corn starch, one and a half cups pastry flour, one-half teaspoonful soda, one and a half teaspoonsful of cream tartar, whites of six eggs.

Wedding Cake.

Twenty-four ounces of sugar, twenty-four ounces of flour, twenty ounces of butter, fifteen eggs, one pound of citron, two pounds of sultana raisins, four pounds of loose muscatels, one ounce of mace, one of allspice, one ounce of cloves, two ounces of cinnamon, one-half pint of brandy. Stone the muscatels, wash the white raisins and dry. Put together as in directions. Bake in a slow oven, and just before it is done pour over it the brandy. This makes it very moist. This cake will keep for years if sealed and kept in a perfectly dry place. This recipe makes a ten-pound loaf. The six pounds of raisins are after they are cleaned.

Dried Apple Cake.

One cup of dried apples soaked over night. Chop fine and add half a cup of molasses and let boil a while slowly. When cool add a cup of brown sugar, one-half cup of butter, half a teaspoon of soda, half a cup of sour milk, teaspoon each of cinnamon, cloves and allspice, two eggs, two cups of flour. Bake in two long tins slowly an hour. A cup of stoned raisins can be added.

☛ Chap-O-Lene will positively cure chapped or rough skin.

Famous Loaf Cake.

Two pounds of raisins, two pounds of currants, one-half a pound of sliced citron. Take one pint of butter and rub into it three quarts of flour and one and one-third pints of sugar; add one pint of milk and three well beaten eggs. One cup of fresh yeast. Mix thoroughly and set to rise. When risen, add a pint more of butter, one and a third of sugar and three eggs; mix and set to rise again. Add the fruit and four grated nutmegs, one-fourth of an ounce of mace, one-fourth of an ounce each of allspice and cloves, one-half an ounce of cinnamon. Let it rise the third time. Bake in a large dripping pan three or four hours. It repays the time and labor employed in making it. Ice it with a boiled icing.

HAVE YOU ASTHMA OR BRONCHITIS?

Dr. R. Shiffmann, St. Paul, Minn., will mail a trial package of "Schiffmann's Asthma Cure" free to any sufferes. He advertises by giving it away. Never fails to give instant relief in worst cases and cures where others fail. Name this Cook Book and send address for a free trial package. Weinhold Drug Co. always keep a supply in stock.

"There's little doubt that courteousness
More dividends than rudeness pays.
See how the gambler gathers in
The dollars by his winning ways."

☞ Caswell's Pectoral Balsam is guaranteed to give satisfaction or money refunded.

TENDERFOOT (to cowboy)—"What do you mean by shooting my dog; he's worth $150?" Cowboy (coolly)—"He ain't now, sonny."

☞ THE lady of the house is requested to read the recipe on page 32.

"CAN'T you wait upon me?" said the impatient customer. "Two pounds of liver; I'm in a hurry." "Sorry," said the butcher; "but there are two or three ahead of you. Surely you would not have your liver out of order!"

☞ ADVERTISERS are requested to read the recipe on page 32.

"IN the Chicago council a flying cuspidor takes precedence over all other motions."

HAVE YOU ASTHMA OR BRONCHITIS?

Dr. R. Schiffmann, St. Paul, Minn., will mail a trial package of "Schiffmann's Asthma Cure" free to any sufferer. He advertises by giving it away. Never fails to give instatnt relief in worst cases and cures where others fail. Name this Cook Book and send address for a free trial package. Weinhold Drug Co. always keep a supply in stock.

"WHAT's that dreadful noise in the parlor, Hannah?" "That do be yer small child amusin' hisself." "What is the darling trying to do?" "He do be makin' a carpet sweeper uv the music-box."

IF listeners wish to hear good of themselves they should practice the art of solliloquizing.—Puck.

☞ WEDDING Invitations, Announcements, At Home, etc. High class work produced by The Swinburne Printing Company, 9-11-13 Washington avenue north.

IMITATION may be the sincerest flattery; but an up-to-date girl does not think so when she is presented with a paste diamond.—Puck.

COOKIES.

COOKIES require a brisk fire. Do not make them too stiff with flour. Sprinkle a little sugar on top before putting in oven. Prepare mixture as for cake. Roll about a quarter of an inch thick. Some press a raisin in the center, or brush them over with a mixture of sugar and water while hot, sprinkle seeds or currents on top and return to oven a moment.

Plain Cookies.

One-half cup of butter, one cup of sugar, one-fourth cup milk, one egg, two even teaspoons baking powder, two cups of flour.

Sour Milk Cookies.

Two cups sugar, one cup of butter, one cup of sour milk, three eggs, one teaspoon soda, mix soft and roll out a quarter of an inch thick.

Jumbles.

One and a half cups of sugar, three-fourths cup butter, three eggs, three tablespoons of sweet milk, half teaspoon of soda, and one of cream tartar. Roll and sprinkle granulated sugar over them.

Hermits.

One-half cup of butter, one and a half cups sugar, one of chopped raisins, two eggs, one teaspoon of soda, two tablespoons of sour milk, one teaspoon each of cinnamon, cloves, and nutmeg.

Hermits. 2.

Two cups of sugar, one cup of butter, one of raisins, (stoned and chopped), three eggs, half teaspoonful of soda in three tablespoons of milk, half a nutmeg, one teaspoon each of cinnamon and cloves, six cupsful of flour. .w

---

☞ Ladies will find Chap-O-Lene an indispensable article for the toilet.

"WELL, did your summer girl meet you at the station with a buggy?"
"No; I had a walk-over."

☞ YOUR attention is respectfully called to page 32.

☞ THE place to get high class printing is at 9-11-13 Washington avenue north.

How to be Happy.

Stop worrying, for it is worry that silvers the hair; worry that bends us to the earth with its cruel and relentless burden. Yes, stop worrying, and when you want a job of printing, no matter how large or how small, go direct to the Swinburne Printing Company, where you can get just what you want, and get it just as you want it. If your time is worth anything, you will save money and be happy every time you follow this receipe.

"WHAT'S THAT?

MY JOB NOT DONE YET!

I ought to have taken it to THE SWINBURNE PRINTING CO. and I'd had it on time. I'll do so hereafter.

The Swinburne Printing Co.

o PRODUCERS OF o

..HIGH-CLASS WORK..

Printing . Binding . Lithographing
Engraving . Embossing

9-11-13 WASHINGTON AVE. N.,
MINNEAPOLIS, MINN.

Ginger Snaps.

One cup of sugar, one cup of molasses, one cup butter, or part butter and lard; tablespoon ginger, teaspoon cinnamon, teaspoon of cloves and allspice, one teaspoonful of soda dissolved in three tablespoons of hot water; flour to roll out easily. Cut small and roll thin. Brown in a quick oven.

Quick Ginger Cakes.

Put one teaspoon of soda in a tea cup, pour on it three tablespoons of boiling water, four tablespoons of melted shortening, fill cup with molasses, add pinch of salt, ginger, cinnamon, etc. to taste. Mix as soft as can be rolled.

Lemon Snaps.

Cup and a half of sugar, two-thirds cup of butter, half teaspoon soda dissolved in two teaspoons hot water. Flavor with lemon, either extract or grated rind and juice of half a lemon. Roll thin.

Alum Ginger Bread.

Pint of molasses, teacup melted shortening, tablespoon of ginger, teacup boiling water; in which dissolve tablespoon of pulverized alum. Take a little of the water and dissolve in it a large tablespoon of soda. Mix soft. Roll about half an inch thick and bake in oblong cards in a quick oven.

Cocoanut Jumbles.

One cup butter, two of sugar, two eggs, one large cup of either grated or desiccated cocoanut. Flour enough to make a dough easily rolled. Bake in a quick oven.

Graham Cookies.

Take two cups maple sugar, one cup butter, one egg, one cup sour milk, teaspoon soda. Mix with Graham flour. Use white flour on the board to roll them out. Brown or white sugar may be used in place of maple.

Seed Cookies.

Cream one-half pound of butter, three-fourths pound sugar, one and one-half pounds of flour, one well beaten egg, half gill rose water, pinch of soda dissolved in tablespoon of warm water. Knead well and bake in a quick oven. Use coriander, caraway or cardamon seeds or any mixture of them preferred.

☞ Use Chap-O-Lene for all roughness of the skin.

THE gallows is not a thing of the past, to judge from the great deal of banging done on Christmas eve.

The Old Reliable

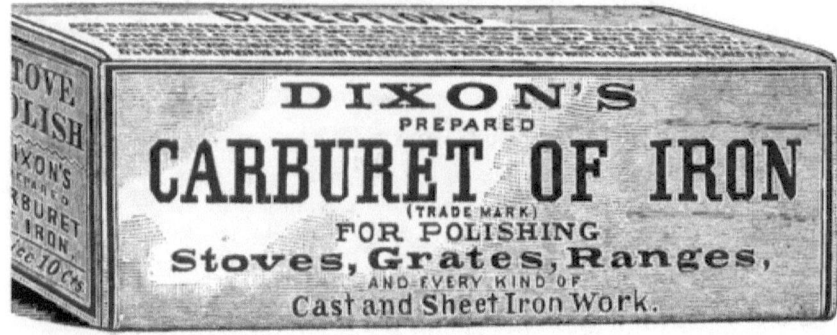

Dixon's Cake Polish does not burn red.
Dixon's Cake Polish does not gum the stove.
Dixon's Cake Polish makes no vile smell.
Dixon's Cake Polish never dries or wastes.
Dixon's Cake Polish is the Cheapest, Neatest, Cleanest.

One Cake of Dixon's

Contains as much polishing matter as **Six Boxes of any Paste Polish.**

Paste Polish is made of **soap, gum** and blacklead. It smears the stove, burns red, rusts the stove and makes **sickening odors.**

Dixon's Cake Polish can be used in similar manner to Paste if desired. Tear off paper on end of cake; rub the Polish on a damp woolen cloth and apply to the stove same as when using Paste Polish. A harder, brighter and more lasting shine is obtained by using a polishing brush after applying with a cloth.

REMEMBER: One Cake of Dixon's Polish is equal to Six Boxes of the Best Paste Polish, and makes no poisonous or vile smells.

JOS. DIXON CRUCIBLE CO.,
JERSEY CITY, N. J.

Established 1827.   Sole Manufacturers.

Sweet Wafers.

Beat one-half a cup of butter to a cream, add gradually one cup of powdered sugar. Beat until smooth and creamy. Beat six eggs light, add them to the butter and sugar, the juice of one lemon and enough flour to make a stiff batter. Bake in wafer iron. If you have none drop the batter by spoonfuls on a greased tin some distance apart, and bake in a quick oven.

Almond Wafers.

Beat one-half of a cup of butter to a cream, add gradually one cup of powdered sugar. Beat six eggs light, and add them to the sugar, add the juice of one lemon, and four ounces of almonds blanched, pounded and chopped. Add flour to make a stiff batter. *y*

A Great Scheme.

Mrs. Goodly—I am willing to give you food if you will work for it.
Weary Wiggins—All right, Madam. I'm willin' ter work at me perfession. I'm de champion pie-eater of America.—Judge.

HAVE YOU ASTHMA OR BRONCHITIS?

Dr. R. Schiffmann, St. Paul, Minn., will mail a trial package of "Schiffmann's Asthma Cure" free to any sufferer. He advertises by giving it away. Never fails to give instatnt relief in worst cases and cures where others fail. Name this Cook Book and send address for a free trial package. Weinhold Drug Co. always keep a supply in stock.

ON a French tombstone—could it have been found on any other?—is the inscription—"Sacred to the memory of Mlle. ——; died April 2, in her eighty-first year. She never looked her age."

☞ How to make Us happy, read the recipe on page 32 and follow it.

THE average young woman does not object to a young man stealing something from under her very nose.—Puck.

Log Cabin Maple Syrup.

LITTLE GIRL—Why do the flies bite so to-day?
Mother—It's going to rain.
Little Girl—Well, they might know 'tain't my fault.—Truth.

☞ Caswell's Beef, Wine and Iron is the Ideal Tonic.

CUSTOMER—"I am troubled with rats in my room." Drggist—"Yes, sir. Bromide or ammonia cocktail?"—Brooklyn Life.

☞ THE housekeeper should not fail to study page 32.

IN Chicago—Wife (nervously)—"Do you think, dear, the cholera will visit us this year?" Husband—"I wouldn't be at all surprised. Everybody else we ever heard of has visited us, and why not the cholera?" Wife (brightening)—"That's so. I hadn't thought of that. I guess we can stand it."—Detroit Free Press.

☞ ARE you going to lay this book down and not read that recipe on page 32.

WANDERING WILLIE—"There is somethin' in that doctrine 'bout castin' yer bread on the waters." Tottering Tom—"Proceed." Wandering Willie—"Why, a cove asked me to hold his coat while he fixed his horse's hoofs, an' I held the coat. Now the coat holds me."—Boston Transcript.

☞ THE only concern in the city making a specialty of high class printing, engraving and embossing is The Swinburne Printing Company.

CANDY.

IN MAKING candy cook over a slow fire. Molasses candy and caramels scorch very quickly. Try by dropping a little in cold water. If it becomes brittle and snaps the candy is hard enough, or test by lifting the spoon, and if the mixture "hairs" or ropes from it, this is a good test that the candy is ready to be removed from the fire. Butter should be put in when the candy is nearly done, and all flavoring should be added just after removing from the fire. A little vinegar or cream of tartar will keep candy from graining. Baker's chocolate should never be allowed to boil, but melted by placing in a pan of hot water on the back of the stove. Never add any water to it.

Cream Candy.

Two cups of white sugar, one-half cup of water. Flavor with vanilla while pulling. Tablespoonful of vinegar. Cook until brittle when dropped in cold water. Cool and pull. Cut in small pieces with the shears.

Cream and Chocolate Candy.

Two cups of granulated sugar, one-half cup of water, one tablespoon of vinegar, one-half teaspoonful of cream of tartar. Flavor with vanilla. Take one-third of the cream and flavor with two tablespoons of grated chocolate. Pour into a mold in layers; dark in center. Cut when partly cold into small cubes.

Butter Scotch.

Two cups of suger, three-quarters of a cup of vinegar, one-half cup of butter. Cook until brittle when dropped in water. Pour in buttered pans, and mark when nearly cold in small squares.

Chocolate Caramels.

One cup grated chocolate, two cups brown sugar, one cup of molasses, large piece of butter, pinch of soda when nearly done. Boil half an hour over a slow fire, as it burns very quickly. Pour in pans, and mark in squares when nearly cold.

☞ Chap-O-Lene will positively cure chapped or rough skin.

Chocolate Drops.

Two and a half cups sugar, one-half cup of water, a pinch of cream of tartar. Boil four minutes, and beat until cold enough to roll into balls with the fingers. Take one-half cake of Baker's chocolate, melt and roll the drops in it, and set them on greased paper to dry. Flavor cream with lemon or vanilla.

Walnut Creams.

Take the above recipe. Make a small ball, and press a walnut meat on both sides, or in place of a walnut use a date.

Almond Macaroons.

Blanch and pound half a pound of almonds to a smooth paste, add a pound of sugar and the whites of three eggs. Work all together. Roll into balls and lay on buttered paper one inch apart. Put in a cool oven three-quarters of an hour.

Molasses Candy.

Two cups Orleans molasses, one cup brown sugar, one tablespoonful of vinegar, piece of butter size of a walnut. Boil until brittle in water. Cool and pull until gold color. Clip off with the shears into pieces an inch long. Flavor the last thing, and add a pinch of soda just before removing from the fire.

Hickory Nut Candy.

Take recipe for molasses candy, and add, just before removing from the fire, one cup of nut meats. Cool in a buttered pan and break up in pieces. Peanuts can be used in place of hickory nut meats.

Lemon Candy.

Take a pound of white sugar, large cup of water. Cook half an hour. Raise spoon, and if it hairs, as we say, it is done. Squeeze in the juice of part of a lemon or a little vinegar and lemon extract. Pour in a tin and mark in squares before it is hard.

Cocoanut Drops.

One cup of powdered sugar, white of an egg, cup of grated or dessicated cocoanut. Roll into little balls and bake on buttered pans.

Nut Candy.

Take the above recipe and pour in just before putting in the pans, chopped cocoanut, almonds, hickory nuts and slices of Brazilian nuts.

MINNEAPOLIS BREWING CO.

LAGER BEER BREWERS.

GENERAL OFFICE AND BREWERY:
CORNER MARSHALL STREET AND 13TH AVENUE N. E.,
MINNEAPOLIS, MINNESOTA.

OUR CELEBRATED BRANDS ARE

Wiener, Kaiser, Lager, Extra Pale.

FAMILY TRADE RECEIVES OUR PARTICULAR ATTENTION.	Keep a Case of our Celebrated Bottled Beer at your Home. It is the Queen of all Table Beers. A glass of it, if taken at meal times, is an excellent strengthener and remedial agent.	ALL ORDERS ARE PROMPTLY ATTENDED TO.

TELEPHONE 1177-2.
RING US UP. . . .

Cocoanut Squares.

One cocoanut grated fine, two cups of milk, butter size of an egg, three pounds of white sugar, two teaspoons of lemon essence. Boil slowly until stiff and pour in two well buttered pans. Mark in squares when partly cold.

Hickory Nut Macaroons.

One egg, half cup of flour, a cup of meats chopped fine, one cup of sugar. Make in balls and bake a few minutes in a slow oven.

Confectionary Candy.

Mix the whites of two eggs and their bulk in water with two pounds of confectionery sugar and a tablespoon of vanilla and lemon mixed. Beat well and you have the foundation for several kinds of candy. For chocolate drops roll into marbles and dip in melted Baker's chocolate, and set up on greased papers to dry. Roll the balls in chopped nut meats or press a walnut on each side of a small piece of the paste and smooth off the rough edges with the fingers and you have a walnut candy. Sprinkle cocoanut on a layer of the paste, roll a little and cut in squares and cocoanut squares are the result. Figs and dates can be used the same as walnuts. This is at present a very popular, cheap and convenient way of making several kinds of candy. It should be eaten at once, as it dries very quickly.

Marrous Glacis.

Purchase large chestnuts, selecting them with great care. Shell and cover with boiling water and let them stand fifteen minutes. Remove the brown skin and cover them with boiling water and let them simmer thirty minutes. Make a syrup of one cup of granulated sugar and one cup of water, add the chestnuts and let them cook slowly until they begin to look clear. Take them out and let them stand one by one on a flat sieve over night. In the morning take one pound of granulated sugar and one cup of water, stir over a fire until the sugar is dissolved, boil until the syrup hairs and then add one teaspoonful of lemon juice, take from the fire and beat, dip the chestnuts in the mixture and put them on greased paper to dry.

☞ THE cook will find something interesting on page 32.

Miss Waldo (of Boston)—"I do love Swinburne. His melody is so—so melodious."
Miss Lakefront (of Chicago)—"Yes, and I do love his odes. They are so odious."
—Phil-adelphia Record.

☞ Gentlemen will find Chap-O-Lene very beneficial applied immediately after shaving.

☞ How to be happy, see page 32.

THE READY FAMILY SOAP MAKER.

LEWIS' 98% LYE!

Powdered and Perfumed.

(PATENTED)

The strongest and purest Lye made. Will make the best Perfumed Hard Soap in 20 minutes *without boiling*.

The best water-softener made. The best disinfectant.

SOME OF THE ADVANTAGES OBTAINED BY USING Lewis' 98 Per Cent. Powdered Lye are:

Unlike other Lye it is packed in an iron can with a removable lid, easily taken off, thereby saving trouble and danger (from flying particles). It being a fine powder, and the lid easily removed, the contents are always ready for use. A teaspoonful can be used in scrubbing, etc., and the lid replaced, saving the balance. With other Lyes all must be used quickly, or the strength is gone. Absolute *purity*. The best soap can be made in from 10 to 20 minutes with this Lye. In making soap no failure is possible if the simple directions are followed. One can is equal to 20 pounds of Washing Soda, is 28 per cent. stronger and will saponify one pound more grease than any other preparation. One teaspoonful will thoroughly cleanse waste pipes, sinks, drains, or closets, and is invaluable for killing insects, etc.

PENNA. SALT MFG. CO.

General Agents, - Philadelphia, Pa.

FOR SALE BY
THE WIENHOLD DRUG CO.

CREAMS AND ICES.

EVERY family should possess a good gallon ice cream freezer. A great many palatable dishes can be made with it in hot weather. The principla feature of making creams and ices is in the freezing. It is essential to have the ice finely crushed. This can be done by first breaking it up into coarse pieces and putting it in a sack made of burlap or some coarse material and pounding with a wooden mallet or an ice cracker. Use one part salt to three parts of ice; rock salt is the best, but coarse salt will do the work. Salt causes the ice to melt rapidly and ice in changing to water absorbs a great deal of heat. This makes the mixture of ice and salt many degrees colder than the ice alone. The outlet to let out the water should be near the top of the eezer. Let it run out as the ice melts, do not drain it off. Put a layer of ice in the bottom of the freezer, then a layer of salt and so on until the freezer is full. Always have the ice come a few inches above the cream in the can. Let the cream or ice stand for eight or ten minutes until chilled, turning occasionally, then rapidly and continuously until the crank begins to turn hard, and you can turn it no longer. It requires from twenty minutes to half an hour to freeze the mixture. Remove the beater and handle, pack down the cream, drain off some of the water, put in a fresh layer of ice and salt and cover with an old sack or piece of carpeting until ready to serve. Cream is better to stand an hour or so before serving. The cream can be removed from the can and packed in fancy shapes or molds; cover the mold closely with a cloth and put the cover on carefully, then pack with fresh ice and salt in some large receptacle. Pour off the water, dip the mold quickly in hot water, turn out on a platter and serve at once. There are many ways of making cream. Cream is the essential element in the best ice cream, but good cream can be made without cream or by using part cream.

Ices and sherbets are made of fruit juices, sugar and water. When made of fruit juice, water and sugar they are called ices. When the white of an egg or a little gelatine is added they are known as sherbets. When cordials or liquors are added to lemon and orange ices they are

Child's Cough Cure is prepared especially for children.

Many Recipes Herein Call for Milk . . . .

Successful results depend largely upon good materials; poor milk may cause entire loss of your labor.

Therefore, Don't Take Chances!!

In all recipes providing for milk and sugar use the celebrated

GAIL BORDEN EAGLE BRAND

Condensed Milk

Always uniform in character, superior to ordinary milk; richer than cream.

If your recipe requires no sweetening then use

BORDEN'S PEERLESS BRAND

Evaporated Cream

A very rich unsweeted Condensed Milk available for every purpose for which ordinary milk is used. It gives better and more uniform results. Directions for use on label of can.

Both Brands are prepared and Guaranteed by the

NEW YORK CONDENSED MILK CO.

FOR SALE BY THE WEINHOLD DRUG CO.

called punches. When a variety of fruit is used the ice is known as macedoines. Sherbets half frozen are called sorbets. When fresh fruit cannot be obtained use the juice of canned fruit; fresh fruit is of course the best. To make ices very rich the juice alone with sugar is used. Adding the white of an egg to a sherbet gives it a creamy consistency; some use a spoonful of gelatine. To make the texture of the ice fine grained boil the sugar and water together; remove the scum and strain. Always sweeten your creams and ices very sweet, more than would be agreeable if not frozen, for the intense coldness deadens the sense of the taste. When lemons are used, grate off some of the rind, squeeze out the juice and let them stand awhile; this gets all the flavor of the lemon. Put in the sugar so as to let that dissolve at the same time, strain and prepare the ice for freezing.

Keep the machinery of the freezer well oiled. Always scald out the can of the freezer before putting it away. Dry the freezer, and drain and dry the salt, as it can be used again. A substitute for a freezer is a covered tin pail placed in a wooden bucket: pack the space around the pail with the ice and salt. Remove cover and stir the cream from the sides occasionally until stiff.

Plain Ice Cream.

Boil one pint of milk and one pint of cream. Beat two eggs very light, add one cup of sugar, a little salt; mix well, and add to the boiling milk. Turn into the double cooker and cook awhile. When cold add two tablespoons of any kind of flavoring. Add more sugar if necessary, and freeze according to directions given.

Quick Ice Cream.

One quart of cream, cup and a half of sugar, pinch of salt, and flavor to taste. Let the sugar stand in the cream awhile so as to dissolve. Beat the whites of two eggs to a stiff froth, put in the bottom of the can and pour in the cream. To make it nice reserve a part of the cream, whip it and add to the rest when it is partly frozen. It will take at least a large tablespoon of flavoring extract.

Neapolitan Ice Cream.

One quart of cream, four eggs, one cup of sugar, flavoring. Scald the cream, beat the yolks, add the sugar, and beat again. Beat whites stiff, and add them to the yolks. Pour in the cream and cook awhile in a double boiler. Strain, and when cold, add flavoring and freeze. With this recipe can be made any variety of cream.

☞ THE Swinburne Printing Company would like to see you when you have any use for printer's ink.

OLDS' WONDERFUL SALVE,

FOR MAN AND BEAST.

It is the greatest discovery of the nineteenth century, and it may be considered

A

well demonstrated fact that it will cure nine-tenths of all local sores on man and beast. Not only that, but it does wonders in curing difficult cases of Eczema, Putrid Ulcers, Old Fever Sores of long standing, well located Syphilitic Sores, and many more ailments too numerous to mention here. It is also a fact that any party who has tried this great Salve once will never be without it, as every man, woman and

CHILD

will testify. For animals (especially horses), it is a positive cure for new or old galls or sores on horses' necks and shoulders where there are no pipes. Apply the Salve freely once in twenty-four hours in the evening after the horse has cooled, and use no water on sore. It is also a certain cure for Scratches and Grease-Heel when taken in time. It is also well known by those engaged in dairy business that it is

FOUND

to be a fact that when this Salve is kept on hand the cows will not kick, for three applications will make the animal perfectly gentle. This great Salve is kept constantly on hand and for sale by Prof. J. P. OLDS. Every box guaranteed to give entire satisfaction or the money will be refunded.

N. B.—All persons who keep this wonderful Salve on hand, and who use it freely before they are

DEAD

are considered safe, and in a favorable way of becoming sound, for

The greatest thing on all creation,
Is a Salve that heals the nation.
So now, my friends, if Sores you have,
Be sure to use this wonderful Salve.

So call on J. P. here in town,
Where at all times he may be found.
Where a free test you all can have,
Of this most wondrous healing Salve.

J. P. Olds we must confess,
Relieves mankind of much distress.
His treatment is so very mild,
It will not harm the smallest child.

Ho! every one that hath a doubt,
Just try one box and you'll find out.
Its healing power will make you shout,
As sure as spots grow on a trout.

I'm sure enough has now been said,
If no one has been found dead,
So come along and get some more
Of this great Salve for every sore.

That man and beast is heir 2,
For it cures nine-tenths of all the sores,
And that is what I'll swear 2.

Price per Ounce Box, 25 cents.   **ASK YOUR DRUGGIST FOR IT.**

J. P. OLDS, Manufacturer and Proprietor, 1409 E. 28th St., Minneapolis.

Always on hand and for sale at wholesale and retail by

THE WEINHOLD DRUG CO.

Chocolate Ice Cream.

Take five tablespoons of grated chocolate, rub smooth in one pint of milk; add two well beaten eggs and two cups of sugar. Beat well and cook in a double boiler until it thickens. When cold flavor with a teaspoon of vanilla. Put in a freezer, and when it begins to set add a quart of rich cream. A cup of preserved peaches cut in small pieces, and added when the cream is almost frozen, makes a delicious cream.

Fruit Frappies.

Line a fancy mold with any nice rich vanilla flavored cream. Fill the center with fresh berries, or peaches, apricots or pears cut in slices. Cover with ice cream. Put in a bucket and pack with ice and salt. Let it stand for an hour. Any kind of berries can be used. Strawberries are the most delicious. If you have not fresh fruit use canned.

Frozen Custard.

Scald one quart of milk. Beat the yolks of four eggs, add one cup of sugar, pinch of salt, and beat well. Place in a double cooker, and cook until creamy. Cool and flavor to taste. This can be made much richer by adding a cup of cream when the custard is partly frozen.

Lemon Ice Cream.

Use any recipe for cream. Neapolitan ice cream is the best. Grate some of the rind of a lemon. Squeeze out the juice. Be careful not to have any of the rind and seeds, as they are apt to give a bitter flavor. Strain and mix with half a cup of sugar. Boil until clear, and stir into the cream just before freezing.

Strawberry Ice Cream.

Take one quart of strawberries and sprinkle a large cup of sugar over them. Mash, and let them stand an hour. Put through a sieve as long as the juice and pulp will come. Put the pulp in a pan and pour on one cup of milk. Strain through a cloth. Add to this one quart of cream, and make it very sweet. Scald the cream and dissolve the sugar in it. The strawberries can be mashed and poured into a quick ice cream when it is partly frozen. Canned strawberries can be used in place of fresh ones.

Raspberry Ice Cream.

Make exactly as the above recipe says, using raspberries in place of strawberries. The juice of a lemon greatly improves it. Raspberries are apt to be too sweet.

1e

Caswell's Pectoral Balsam is a perfect cough cure.

Banana Ice Cream.

Peel six ripe bananas, remove the dark seeds and the dark line in the centre. Rub the pulp through a strainer and add sugar to make it very sweet. A little lemon juice improves it. Add a pinch of salt, and put in any ice cream, made from the preceding recipes, when partly frozen, or make one as follows: One quart of cream, one cup of sugar and flavor to taste. Prepare as in quick ice cream.

Peach Ice Cream.

Take a dozen large, ripe freestone peaches, pare and chop; add a few of the stone meats. Add large cup of sugar to the peaches and let them stand awhile. Wash the pulp through a sieve and stir in any kind of ice cream. The peaches can be used without putting them through a strainer.

Apricot Ice Cream.

Take a quart of apricots, add one cup of sugar and let them stand awhile; then rub the pulp through a sieve. Scald one quart of cream and add one cup of sugar to it; cool and put in a freezer. Add the beaten white of an egg and the apricot pulp. Freeze according to directions.

Maraschino Ice Cream.

Make a Neapolitan ice cream, flavor with vanilla and almond flavoring. When ready to serve pour three spoonfuls of maraschino over the cream.

Pistachio Ice Cream.

Shell, blanch and pound one-quarter of a pound of pistachio nuts, add half a cup of almond meats chopped and pounded to a paste. Make a plain ice cream or any kind, flavor with a teaspoonful of vanilla and almond mixed, and add the nuts and almonds. Freeze as usual. The nuts can be used alone without the almonds, or use the almonds alone and call it almond ice cream. Pistachio ice cream can be colored the desired shade by using spinach coloring.

Tutti Frutti Ice Cream.

Make a quick ice cream, flavor with a little Madeira or any rich wine. Take a mixture of candied fruit, using plums, cherries, pears, strawberries and apricots, about a pound in all. Cut up fine and add to the cream when partly frozen.

"YOUR husband is so magnetic a man," said the visitor. "I know it," responded the wife. "I found a steel hairpin sticking to his coat collar the other day."—Washington Star.

☞ HIGH class printing, engraving and embossing at 9-11-13 Washington avenue north.

Hickory Nut Ice Cream.

Take a pint of hickory nut kernels, pick over carefully, pound in a mortar. Put two tablespoons of sugar over the fire without water, stir until browned; add a little water to dissolve it, add it to the nuts. Take one quart of cream and sweeten one teacup and a half of ice cream, add the nut paste and freeze.

New York Ice Cream.

Take one quart of cream, one teacup and a half of sugar and a tablespoon of vanilla. Beat the yolks of six eggs and pour the boiling cream on them; put over the fire for a minute. Freeze. This, molded with chocolate and lemon ice cream, is very nice.

Nut Ice Cream.

Take filberts, chestnuts or English walnuts; American walnuts, hickory nuts and pecans can be used. Shell, blanch if necessary; chop or pound to a paste, and stir in any plain ice cream. In using pecans avoid getting any of the puckery substance which adheres to the meat.

Fruit Cream.

One-half can of apricots, three bananas, three oranges, three cups of sugar, two lemons and three cups of water. Prepare the fruit as given in the other recipes. Pour on the water and sugar, let it stand awhile. Put all the pulp through a strainer, add more sugar if necessary. Mix with the fruit a cup of rich cream, or one pint, and freeze. This is delicious. If canned fruit is used, rub through a strainer and add one quart of whipped cream. For canned fruit use peaches, apricots, cherries, strawberries, etc.

Nesselrode Pudding.

One-half a pint of shelled almonds, one pint of shelled chestnuts, a pint of canned pineapple. Boil the chestnuts half an hour and pound to a paste; blanch the almonds and pound the same as the chestnuts; boil the pineapple with one pint of water and one pint of sugar twenty minutes. Add the yolks of five eggs, well beaten, put in a dish of boiling water and beat until it thickens. Add the nuts and half a pound of French candied fruit cut up fine, to one pint of cream. Mix with the cooked mixture. Flavor and add a pinch of salt. Freeze and mold the same as ice cream.

A JUDGE in Ohio has sentenced a man to be hanged before daybreak. This may not be cruel or unusual punishment in the case of a farm-hand, but it would be rough on most other citizens who do not care to have their sleep broken.—Buffalo Express.

☞ Ladies will find Chap-O-Lene an indispensable article for the toilet.

THE WEINHOLD DRUG CO.

BURNISHINE.

THE MOST MARVELOUS METAL POLISH IN THE WORLD.

Its Action is Wonderful. Will produce a most Brilliant Luster to Brass, Copper, Zinc, Steel, Tin, Bronze, Gold, Silver and all Metals.

Half a Dozen Rubs and the Article is Handsomely Burnished.

Will not injure Gold or Silver and is excellent for polishing household articles.

Will restore burnt or rusty nickel on stoves to its original luster.

Warranted Strictly not to Contain Acids.

BURNISHINE will not soil your hands or leave deposits in corners of the metal, like paste polish does.

Beware of imitations put up in packages similar to ours.

Put up in
4 oz. Bottles.
Half Pint Cans.
One Pint Cans.
Quart Cans.
Half Gal. Cans.
One Gal. Cans.

J. C. PAUL & CO., Sole Mnfrs.

OFFICE:
121 Lake Street.

FACTORY:
1414-1416 Roscoe Street.

CHICAGO, ILL.

Frozen Pudding.

Make two quarts of rich boiled custard, add two tablespoons of gelatine dissolved in half a cup of cold milk. Add to the custard and when it is just beginning to freeze add one pound of raisins, one pint fruit preserves, one quart of whipped cream. Almonds and grated cocoanut make the pudding nice but can be left out.

Lemon Ice.

Two quarts of water, two pounds of sugar, juice of half a dozen lemons grate off some of the rind, squeeze out the juice and pour the water hot on the lemons. Strain; and add the sugar; when cold freeze the same as cream, add the well beaten whites of three eggs and you have lemon sherbet.

Orange Sherbet.

Make the same as lemon, using ten oranges and the whites of six eggs. The juice and rind of two lemons greatly improve it.

Pineapple Sherbet.

Take one pint of fresh or one can of grated pineapple. If a fresh pineapple is used it will take one; pare, dig out the eyes and reject the hard core, chop or grate; add two cups of sugar, two cups of water and one lemon; soak the gelatine in a little cold water and then dissolve in boiling water, add the whites of two eggs and freeze. The egg can be omitted; a little orange juice and pulp improves the flavor. Use one tablespoon of gelatine.

Pineapple Ice.

One can of grated pineapple, one cup and a half of sugar and one pint and a half of water; pour the juice from the cans in a bowl, put the fruit with half the water and cook twenty minutes; put the sugar in the remainder of the water and boil; rub the cooked pineapple through a sieve and add the boiling syrup. Cook a few minutes longer, add the juice and cool and freeze.

Raspberry Sherbet.

One pint of berry juice, two cups of sugar, two cups of water, juice of one lemon, one tablespoonful of gelatine ; mash and put the berries through a sieve, add sugar and gelatine already dissolved and freeze. In place of the gelatine use the beaten whites of two eggs.

Strawberry Sherbet.

Make this the same as raspberry, using a little more sugar. If canned fruit is used use half as much sugar.

KNOWLEDGE

Brings comfort and improvement and tends to personal enjoyment when rightly used. The many, who live better than others and enjoy life more, with less expenditure, by more promptly adapting the world's best products to the needs of physical being, will attest the value to health of the pure liquid laxative principles embraced in the remedy, Syrup of Figs.

Its excellence is due to its presenting in the form most acceptable and pleasant to the taste, the refreshing and truly beneficial properties of a perfect laxative; effectually cleansing the system, dispelling colds, headaches and fevers and permanently curing constipation It has given satisfaction to millions and met with the approval of the medical profession, because it acts on the Kidneys, Liver and Bowels without weakening them and it is perfectly free from every objectionable substance.

Syrup of Figs is for sale by all druggists in 50 cent bottles, but it is manufactured by the California Fig Syrup Co. only, whose name is printed on every package, also the name, Syrup of Figs, and being well informed, you will not accept any substitute if offered,

Frozen Strawberries.

Take two quarts of fresh strawberries, two cups of sugar, one quart of water; boil sugar and water together, add the strawberries and cook a few minutes; cool and when frozen, add one pint of whipped cream. This makes a delicious dessert. If canned strawberries are used, use half as much sugar and do not cook.

Frozen Raspberries.

Prepare the same as strawberries; when cold add the juice of two lemons and freeze; add the whipped cream. Any kind of fruit or berries can be prepared in this way.

Currant or Cherry Ice.

Take one pint of currant and cherry juice, add one pint of water and one pound of sugar; boil sugar and water together, then add the fruit juice, strain and freeze; add more sugar if one likes it very sweet.

Bonanza Punch.

Beat two eggs light and creamy, add two tablespoons of sugar and beat again; add two tablespoons of wine or brandy and one cup of cream or milk. Put in a freezer and turn until half frozen.

Roman Punch.

Take the juice and rind of five lemons, two large cups of sugar and one quart of water. Boil the sugar and water together, add the grated rind and juice of the lemons; strain; through a cloth and flavor with half a cup of good rum. Brandy can be used. The beaten whites of two eggs make it smooth and creamy.

Claret Punch.

Prepare the same as for Roman punch. Use a little more sugar and one-half a pint of good claret; more can be added if desired.

Wine Punch.

Half lemon and half orange juice, flavored with any kind of nice wine, makes a nice punch. Sweeten to taste.

HAVE YOU ASTHMA OR BRONCHITIS?

Dr. R. Shiffmann, St. Paul, Minn., will mail a trial package of "Schiffmann's Asthma Cure" free to any sufferes. He advertises by giving it away. Never fails to give instant relief in worst cases and cures where others fail. Name this Cook Book and send address for a free trial package. Weinhold Drug Co. always keep a supply in stock.

"CALLED down"—The feathers on an elder duck.—Chicago Record.

We Always Recommend : : :

BROMO SELTZER,

FOR HEADACHE,

Because it INVARIABLY Cures all kinds of

Headaches, Neuralgia, Nervousness

AND

Nervous Dyspepsia.

Prices 10, 25 and 50 cents, at all of our Stores.

YOUR ORDERS SOLICITED.

Weinhold Drug Co.,
MINNEAPOLIS, MINN.

CREAMS AND CUSTARDS.

FOR creams and custards, beat the yolks and the whites of the eggs separately. Use an earthen bowl. When gelatine is used, soak in a little cold water for awhile, and dissolve in the hot mixture just after it is removed from the stove. To make a good boiled custard the rule is, the yolks of three eggs to a pint of milk, and three tablespoons of sugar, or four eggs, one cup of sugar to every quart of milk. Always heat the milk in a double cooker, then add the sugar, and lastly the eggs. This keeps it from curdling. Flavor when cool. Use eggs that are strictly fresh, as nothing will taste so quickly in a cream as a packed egg. In baking custards, bake in a very slow oven until firm in the centre. If the oven is too hot the custard will turn to whey. The only spices to be used must be cinnamon and nutmeg. The best charlotte russe is made of well whipped cream as a filling. A great many people use gelatine. Cream intended for whipping should be first chilled on the ice, and sweetened after it is partly whipped. Use an egg beater. Flavor the last thing. If the cream does not whip well add the white of an egg and whip with it. Do not whip it too long or it will turn to butter. Gelatine is put up in two-ounce packages. When the recipe calls for half a package one ounce should be used. One pint of cream will make three times as much whipped cream.

Sherry Cream.

One pint of rich cream, one cup of sherry wine, one cup of lemon (grated rind and juice), one cup of sugar, whites of two eggs beaten light. Whip the cream, add eggs and wine. Serve in glasses with the froth of the cream on top.

Charlotte Russe.

One pint of cream, one teaspoon of vanilla, one-half cup of sugar. Place the bowl containing the cream in cold water, whip to a stiff froth. Skim off the froth and strain. Whip again and repeat it. Line a pudding dish with slices of stale sponge cake, or dry lady fingers. Cover with the cream, and put pieces of currant or wine jelly on top. Put in a cold place until ready to serve.

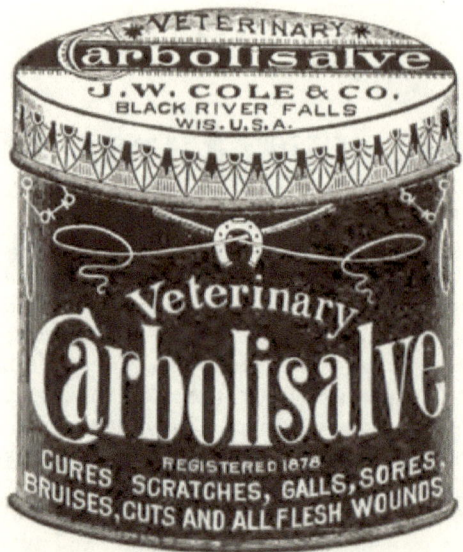

THE GREAT HORSE AND CATTLE REMEDY.

COLE'S VETERINARY CARBOLISALVE

Is a Perfect Remedy for all abrasions of the skin and diseases of the Feet of Horses and Cattle.

It heals sores quickly and permanently, *and is the only remedy that invariably renews the hair its original color.*

It toughens the feet, keeps the frog soft and healthy and is the best hoof grower known.

It will Cure any case of Scratches, Speed Crack or Cracked Heel.

This preparation contains no animal fats, is not affected by exposure to the atmosphere, and will never become rancid. It will not gum the collar or pads.

Flies will never trouble a sore upon which it is used.

Cole's Veterinary Carbolisalve is used and indorsed by the leading horsemen and stockmen of this country.

Large Cans, $1.00.   Small Cans, 50 cents.

J. W. COLE & CO., Sole Proprietors,
Black River Falls, Wis., U. S. A.

Charlotte Russe.

Take one ounce of gelatine, and dissolve in half a cup of of boiling milk; whites of four eggs beaten to a stiff froth, a cup and a half of sugar, and one pint of thick cream whipped to a froth. Mix the gelatine, sugar and whipped cream, add the whites of the eggs. Line a mold with slices of spongecake. Put a layer of jelly over the cake. Cover with the cream and put on the ice until ready to serve. A cup of wine can be added for extra flavoring. If wine is used, use double the amount of gelatine.

Whipped Cream.

Place a pint of cream on the ice until it is chilled through. Whip with an egg-beater until it froths. Skim off the froth on a sieve, strain and return to the bowl. Whip until the cream is stiff. If it does not whip well, add the white of an egg. This can be served sweetened and flavored, with baked apples, fresh fruit or jelly.

Chocolate Bavarian Cream.

One pint of cream, one cupful of milk, half a cup of sugar, half a box of gelatine, one square of chocolate. Soak the gelatine in half of the milk. Melt the chocolate in two tablespoons of water and stir until glossy; add the remainder of the milk, heated to the boiling point. Add gelatine. Strain and add the sugar. Put in a cool place and beat until it thickens. Add the pint of cream whipped to a stiff froth, sweetened and flavored a little.

Orange Cream.

One pint of cream, juice of three oranges and a little of the grated rind, a cup of sugar, the yolks of three eggs, one ounce of gelatine. Soak the gelatine in half a cup of cold water. Grate the rind and squeeze the juice of the oranges in the gelatine. Strain, and add the sugar. Take half the cream and put it in a double boiler; add the yolks to the milk. Stir, and when it begins to thicken, add the gelatine. When it begins to cool add the orange juice and sugar. Beat and add the remainder of the cream. Put in molds and serve with whipped cream.

Log Cabin Maple Syrup.

A CHICAGO school-teacher favors the readers of a current magazine with his views on "What a Daily Newspaper Might Be Made." In the vernacular, it appears he would make a monkey of it.—Chicago Times.

☞Caswell's Pectoral Balsam is guaranteed to give satisfaction or money refunded.

☞DON'T skip page 32, as it contains something of interest to you.

: SPECIAL FOR LADIES. :

PIMPLES AND ROUGHNESS CURED.

A Soft Velvety Skin and Clear Complexion.

HEALTH, ◆ TONE, ◆ VIGOR.

ALICE J. SHAW, of Her Majesty's Theatre, Haymarket, London, says:
"I have used Microbe Killer for a considerable time and found it the finest tonic the world has ever produced. And it has no equal, and I would not be without it for many times its cost."

A. H. CHAMBERLAIN, (Dentist to the Court of Italy), 53 Harley St., Cavendish Square, W. London, says:
"I have thoroughly tested the Radam Microbe Killer as a tonic and cleanser, and found it the best I have ever seen; also a splendid thing for the teeth."

Dr. LESLIE E. KEELEY, says:
"The ferment of the microbe in the body underlies all diseases. A cure will be found in the discovery of some single remedy which will destroy the microbes."

RADAM'S MICROBE KILLER IS THE CURE.

SICK HEADACHE, BACKACHE,

All those IRREGULARITIES known as female trouble are cured by

RADAM'S MICROBE KILLER,

A Pleasant, Refreshing and Healthful Drink.

—— OFFICES ——

325 Hennepin Ave., **MINNEAPOLIS.**   18 East 4th Street, **ST. PAUL.**

☞ Pamphlet and special circular for Ladies given or sent on application.

Peach Bavarian Cream.

A can of best peaches, mash and rub them through a sieve. Put them in a saucepan and let them cook slowly a few minutes. Add an ounce of gelatine soaked in a half cup of water. Add a cup of sugar. Remove from the fire and beat until it commences to thicken. Stir in a cup of cream. Serve with whipped cream. Pineapple cream can be made the same way by using a can of pineapple. Rub as much of the pineapple as you can through a sieve. A pint of cream can be added in place of a cupful. The pineapple should be chopped fine before it is put on to cook in the water. Pineapple makes a delicious cream. Use pears and apricots in the same way.

Tapioca Cream.

Soak two tablespoons of tapioca in one-half teacup of milk. Heat a quart of milk, add half a teacup of sugar and the well beaten yolks of three eggs; add tapioca and stir all together; boil a few minutes, turn into a dish and spread on the well beaten whites of the eggs; flavor the cream with vanilla. It is a good plan to cook the tapioca in the water it is soaked in until clear before adding it to the milk. This is nice poured over stale slices of sponge cake, and served with pieces of jelly laid around on the frosting.

Blanc Mange.

Take three heaping tablespoons of corn starch and dissolve in a little milk; beat three eggs, add three tablespoons of sugar, heat one quart of milk to the boiling point, stir in the starch and lastly the eggs and sugar; flavor to suit the taste, pour in a mold and serve with sweetened cream flavored with vanilla; place teaspoonful of jelly on each plate.

Apple Snow.

Cook six tart apples in as little water as possible, cool and strain; whip the whites of three eggs well, add to the apple and a half cup of sugar, flavor with lemon or vanilla or the grated rind and juice of a lemon, beat well and serve with whipped cream, or pour on a custard and serve cold.

Fruit Blanc Mange.

Take either raspberries or strawberries and stew and strain the juice; sweeten to taste and to every pint of juice add two tablespoons of cornstarch; when cooked so that it is thick pour in molds and serve with either cream and sugar or whipped cream.

☞ IF you are going to be married read page 32.

An Old Family Recipe.

FIFTY YEARS STANDING.

ECZEMA, SALT RHEUM, ERYSIPELAS, PIMPLES, AND ALL SCROFULOUS ERUPTIONS.

—— Cured by ——

"SKIN·SUCCESS"
(TRADE MARK REGISTERED)

THIS Ointment is an old family remedy that has been selling quietly for over 50 years. During this period it has been thoroughly tested in thousands of cases of SKIN diseases, so that now IT is positively GUARANTEED to cure.

Every Doctor or Druggist in the country is politely CHALLENGED to produce a case that "SKIN-SUCCESS" OINTMENT cannot cure.

Trial size box, 25 cts. Large box, 75 cts. At all druggists, or sent by mail upon receipt of price.

"Skin-Success" Soap for

THIS SOAP contains pure Ext. Witch Hazel. Cures Dandruff and relieves all Irritation and Chafing. Grand for Shampooing and general toilet use 25 cents a cake.

The Babies

THE MORGAN DRUG CO.
1512 and 1514 Atlantic Ave., Brooklyn, N. Y.

Orange Souffle.

A pint of milk, three eggs, one-fourth of a cup of sugar; grate in a little of the orange peel for a flavor, beat the yolks of the eggs with the sugar, pour the boiling milk over this and cook in a double boiler until it thickens; peel four sweet oranges, take out the seeds and slice, put in a pudding dish and sprinkle sugar over them and let them stand while the custard is cooling. Pour on the cold custard and add the whites beaten to a stiff froth and sweetened; brown in a very hot oven or under the blaze in the oven of a gas range.

Candied Fruit Cream.

Soak one-half a box of gelatine in one-half a cup of cold water. Chill and whip one pint of cream, after taking off the froth and straining, as given in the directions for whipped cream; boil what is left in the bowl with milk enough to make a pint in all, add half a cup of sugar and when boiling the gelatine strain into the well beaten whites of three eggs; flavor with vanilla and a large tablespoon of wine; when this thickens add the whipped cream, stir in one cup of mixed French fruit. Pour in a mold and garnish with jelly. Nuts like almonds and pisthachio can be added.

Cheese Souffle.

Melt a tablespoon of butter, stir in two tablespoons of flour and a little milk. Season with salt, pepper and a grain of cayenne. Take from the fire and stir in the yolks of three eggs and a cup of grated cheese. Beat thoroughly, then add the beaten whites of the eggs. Bake in cups in a hot oven. Serve as soon as they are done in the cups.

Apple Charlotte.

Soak one-third of a box of gelatine in one-third of a cup of cold water. Pour half a cup of boiling water on it and stir until dissolved. Cook apples enough to make a pint when rubbed through the sieve. Pour on the gelatine and add one cup of sugar and the juice of a lemon. Beat until it thickens, then add the whites of three eggs beaten stiff. Beat well and pour into a mold lined with lady fingers or sponge cake. Serve either with whipped cream or make a soft custard of the yolks of the eggs.

☞ ANYTHING from a calling card to a large show card embossed in colors, or from a circular to a history of the world, can be produced by the Swinburne Printing Company, 9-11-13 Washington avenue north.

AN authority on the just proportions of the human form, divine or otherwise, says, "The ears should be so placed as not to be higher than the eyebrows or lower than the tip of the nose." People who are dressing for a party should not forget this.—Drake's Magazine.

☞ Caswell's Blood Cleaner will purify the blood.

Phœnix Mill Company,

SUCCESSORS TO

STAMWITZ & SCHULER,

MANUFACTURERS OF

The **BEST FLOUR** Made for Family Use.

FOR **CLEARNESS** IN **COLOR**, **RICHNESS** IN **TASTE**, AND **ABUNDANCE** IN **QUALITY**, THERE IS NONE LIKE

PHŒNIX BEST
—— OR ——
WHITE LILY.

These Flours Received the Gold Medal at World's Fair.
All Grocers keep them.

A Nice Dessert.

Put in a deep bowl pieces of stale cake. Cut in squares or strips. Cut up a small piece of preserved citron and put in with the cake. Pour a little cream over this and let the cake soak awhile. Fill the bowl with a boiled custard and on top either place whipped cream or the whites of eggs. Cover with bits of fruit or jelly and serve cold.

Cup Custards.

One pint of milk, two well beaten eggs, one small cup of sugar. Stir together and pour into cups. Set the cups in boiling water in the oven. Bake twenty minutes. Serve in the cups with a slice of jelly on top or a little dessicated cocoanut sprinkled over the top of the cream in each cup.

1n

HAVE YOU ASTHMA OR BRONCHITIS?

Dr. R. Schiffmann, St. Paul, Minn., will mail a trial package of "Schiffmann's Asthma Cure" free to any sufferer. He advertises by giving it away. Never fails to give instant relief in worst cases and cures where others fail. Name this Cook Book and send address for a free trial package. Weinhold Drug Co. always keep a supply in stock.

"I want a realistic work," she said
With such a tender look.
The wealthy banker, with a bow,
Gave her his pocket-book.
—Detroit Free Press.

☞ Caswell's Pectoral Balsam cures all coughs, colds and affections of the throat, chest and lungs.

"What is the lesson taught us in the parable of the seven wise virgins?" asked a Sunday-school teacher of his pupils. "That we should always be on the lookout for a bridegroom," said the smallest girl in the class.—Texas Siftings.

☞ Every business man can profit if he will carefully follow the recipe on page 32.

What Blocked the Railroad.

"Business was blocked on the Sixth Avenue Elevated for nearly an hour this morning."
"What was the matter—a fire?"
"No; but five girls stood before the ticket-window at Fourteenth street while they settled which of them should pay the fare."—Truth.

☞ Your attention is respectfully called to page 32.

Prendergast has not yet announced a lecture course, but if this foolery of insanity talk gets into the heads of jurors we may yet be treated to a sight of this choice specien informming the gaping public (for consideration)"Why I Killed Carter Harrison."—Elmira Advertiser.

☞ We guarantee our work. If it is not entirely satisfactory send it back; don't use it up and then ask for a rebate, as you won't get it. We don't care to deal with cranks. The Swinburne Printing Company.

Dix—If my wife asks you my brand of cigars between now and Christmas, tell her these, and say—
Dealer—Yes.
Dix—Don't charge her over $1 a box; I'll pay the balance.—Truth.

☞ Wedding Invitations, Announcements, At Home, etc. High class work produced by The Swinburne Printing Company, 9-11-13 Washington avenue north.

Towle's "Log Cabin" Maple Syrup.

Absolutely Pure and Full Measure.

$500 offered for any adulteration found in this brand of Maple Syrup.

THE TOWLE SYRUP CO.,
FAIRFAX, VT.   ST. PAUL, MINN.

TOWLE'S
Self-Raising Griddle Cake Flour
...AND...
Towle's Self-Raising Buckwheat Flour

are made from strictly pure material, and guaranteed to give satisfaction, or **MONEY REFUNDED**. Either of the above brands are more wholesome, and more economical to the consumer, than buying the flour in bulk, and making in the old-fashioned way of raising ovre night. Both of the above are prepared and ready for use at a moment's notice, and require no **YEAST, BAKING POWDER OR SALT**. Ask your grocer for the above brands and take no others.

DOUGHNUTS AND CRULLERS.

IN MAKING doughnuts never mix hard. Using eggs prevents them from soaking the fat. Roll about half an inch thick, cut with cookie cutter and cut out the center with some round article about one-fourth as large. An iron kettle is the best for frying. Use best leaf lard, or half lard and the drippings from beef suet. Cottosuet is an excellent substitute for either. When the fat is first used clarify with slices of raw potato. Let them fry for a few minutes and then skim them out. By cooling and straining the fat can be used a second time. Have the fat boiling hot. If hot enough it will cease to bubble. Try by dropping in a small piece of your dough; if it rises in a few seconds and browns on the under side quickly it is just right. Put in the doughnuts or crullers and turn as they rise to the top of the fat. Fry a light brown; try with a steel fork. If the fork comes out clean, drain over the kettle and place in a large pan a short distance apart. Sprinkle powdered sugar over them and keep in a stone jar; this keeps them moist.

Good Doughnuts.

One cup of sugar, three tablespoons of butter, melted, or take equal parts of butter and lard, cup and a half of buttermilk, or sour milk, level teaspoon of soda, pinch of salt, one-half a teaspoon of ginger and cinnamon, one egg. Let them stand for couple of hours and rise.

Raised Doughnuts.

One half cup sugar, one-half cup of butter and lard mixed (make this a small half cup), one egg, one cup of sweet milk, one-half cup of yeast, or one-half a cake of compressed yeast, one-fourth teaspoon of soda, one-fourth teaspoon each of salt, ginger and cinnamon. Mix over night and keep warm. Cut out in the morning and let them rise on the board for an hour.

Doughnuts.

One egg, cup of sweet milk, one cup of sugar, tablespoon of melted butter, pint and a half of flour, two teaspoons of baking powder, a little cinnamon and nutmeg. Mix soft and fry at once.

☞ THE place to get high class printing is at 9-11-13 Washington avenue north.

Crullers.

One tablespoon of melted butter, two heaping tablespoons of sugar, one egg, one-half salt spoon of salt, one-half salt spoon of cinnamon or mace. Roll quarter of an inch thick, cut in squares. Make three or four incisions in each square; lift by taking alternate pieces between the finger and thumb; fold together slightly in the middle and drop into hot fat, and fry like doughnuts.

Crullers.

Three tablespoons of melted butter, half a cup of sugar, three eggs, two tablespoons of sweet milk, half a teaspoon of soda, teaspoonful of cream of tartar, a little ginger or nutmeg.

Wonders.

One egg, pinch of salt, flour to make a very stiff batter. Roll thin as a wafer and cut with a large cutter. Serve with cream or maple syrup.

Fried Corn-meal Cakes.

One pint of milk, poured boiling hot upon one cup of corn-meal; add one heaping tablespoon of sugar, a little salt. Let it stand all night, then add two eggs and half a cup of flour. Fry in hot lard.

Fried Rye Muffins.

One pint of sour milk, one-half cup of molasses, pinch of salt, salt spoon of cinnamon, one teaspoon of soda, two eggs. Rye flour to make a stiff drop batter. Fry in hot lard.

Fried Flour Muffins.

One egg, one-half cup of sugar, three-fourths cup of milk, one teaspoonful of baking powder, salt spoon of salt, flour enough to make a stiff batter. Fry like doughnuts.

1p

To a Lady I Know.

Oh, hearken, I pray, to this little rhyme,
And judge of its pro and its con:
You may stop the clock, but the wheel of time
Rolls surely, cruelly on!—Judge.

☞ THE lady of the house is requested to read the recipe on page 32.

HE—Humph! I am going to marry money.
She—Then I should think you would have to get up a more intimate acquaintance with it than you have at present.—Truth.

☞ ADVERTISERS are requested to read the recipe on page 32.

"THIS child," said the clergyman, who was about to Christen Brown's baby, "may some day make a noise in the world."
And the next minute when Master Brown felt the cold water, the good man's prophesy was verefied more speedily than he had expected.—Truth.

EGGS.

LET me say at the start, that the most to be said about eggs is, that the fresher they are the better they are and the more wholesome. Never buy eggs the freshness of which you have any doubt. If eggs appear heavy and dark, or if they gurgle when shaken, they are bad. When eggs are put in a vessel to cook, if they lie on their sides they are apt to be good; but if they stand on end and float on top of the water, reject them at once. This is explained by the fact that the shells being very porous, on exposure to the air the water inside evaporates, eggs grow lighter, and air rushing into them to take the place of the water, decomposition takes place. Eggs are the most nutritious of food. Do not economize in the use of them. Hard boiled and fried eggs are the hardest to digest. Eggs with dark shells are the richer, as the yolks which contain the nutriment are larger. Eggs to be soft require three minutes; hard, five minutes. In poaching an egg add a little vinegar. This keeps the white of the egg from spreading. Eggs are prepared in an unlimited variety of styles. They make good dishes for breakfast and lunch and are indispensible in cakes, puddings and desserts. Do not have the water quite boiling when the egg is first put in, as it is not so apt to crack as when the water is boiling. In poaching or frying an egg, first break them carefully into a saucer and slip them gently into the water or hot fat. In making omelets beat the yolks and whites separately.

Boiled Eggs.

Put the eggs in a pan, cover with hot water and let them stand about ten minutes where the water will keep hot, but not boil. Serve at once, as they soon harden in the shell, or put them on in cold water and when the water boils the eggs will be done. If the eggs are to be very soft, let them stand in the hot water only five minutes.

Hard Boiled Eggs.

Cook the eggs twenty minutes in water below the boiling point. If the yolk is cooked ten minutes it will be tough; if cooked twenty, mealy and easily reduced to a powder.

A Skin of Beauty is a Joy Forever.

DR. T. FELIX GOURAUD'S
ORIENTAL CREAM
OR
MAGICAL BEAUTIFIER

Purifies as well as Beautifies the Skin.

No other Cosmetic will do it.

Removes Tan, Pimples, Freckles, Moth-Patches, Rash and Skin diseases, and every blemish on beauty, and defies detection. On its virtues it has stood the test of forty-three years; no other has; and is so harmless we taste it to be sure it is properly made. Accept no counterfeit of similar name. The distinguished Dr. L. A. Sayre, said to a lady of the *hautton* (a patient): "*As you ladies will use them, I recommend 'Gouraud's Cream' as the least harmful of all the Skin preparations.*" One bottle will last six months, using it every day. Also Poudre Subtile removes superfluous hair without injury to the skin.

FERD T. HOPKINS, Prop'r, 37 Great Jones St., N. Y.

For sale by all Druggists and Fancy Goods Dealers throughout the U. S., Canadas and Europe.

Also found in N. Y. City at R. H. Macy's, Stearn's, Ehrich's, Ridley's, and other Fancy Goods Dealers. ☞ Beware of Base Imitations. $1,000 Reward for arrest and proof of any one selling the same.

Dropped Eggs.

Break the eggs one by one in a saucer and slip into boiling water for a few minutes, about three. Pour off the water and take out carefully, season with salt and pepper and little bits of butter. Serve on slices of toast or on pieces of broiled ham. Instead of pouring off the water, if you have any more to cook take each up with a skimmer.

Poached Eggs.

Break the eggs in hot salted water for two minutes, pour off the water and beat the eggs. Season with salt, pepper and a little butter. Serve on toast at once.

Baked Eggs.

Put six eggs in a dish in the bottom of which has been placed bits of butter, pepper and salt, and pour over them three tablespoons of cream. Set in a hot oven and bake fifteen minutes. Serve at once.

Ham Omelet.

Take bits of either boiled or fried ham, chop fine. Put in a frying pan with a large piece of butter. Pour over the ham four well beaten eggs. Season with salt and pepper and stir all together. Cook until brown, and turn over carefully and brown on the other side.

Scalloped Eggs.

Boil six eggs twenty minutes. Moisten a cup of cracker crumbs in a little butter or cream; chop fine bits of ham, chicken or fish; about one cup in all. Remove the yolks and chop the whites. Put a layer of the crumbs in the bottom of a dish, then the chopped whites, minced meat, yolks rubbed to a powder, and so on until the dish is full; finish with a layer of crumbs. Pour over it a pint of white sauce or stock and milk enough to moisten well. Bake until brown.

Scalloped Eggs.

Cover a buttered dish with fine bread or cracker crumbs. Put each egg carefully in the dish; about six. Season with salt and pepper, and butter and cover with a layer of bread crumbs. Bake until the crumbs are brown in a hot oven. Instead of using a large dish use cups, and prepare the eggs in the same way by dropping one egg in each cup.

☞ Use Chap-O-Lene for all roughness of the skin.

☞ ☞ THE lady of the house is requested to read the recipe on page 32.

☞ Ladies will find Chap-O-Lene an indispensable article for the toilet.

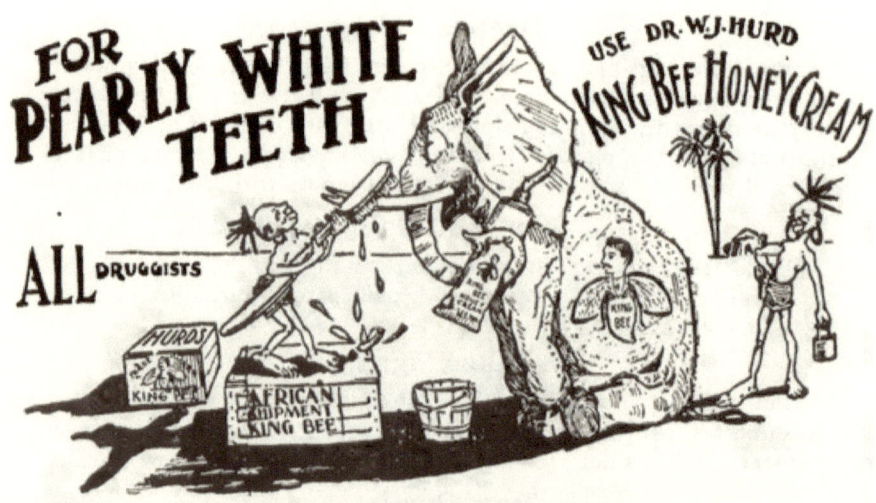

FOR CLEANING THE TEETH.

Contains the best known compositions for neutralizing the acids of the mouth, preventing deposits on the teeth, which causes them to decay and become loosened.

The loss of the teeth is soon followed by ill health, so it behooves everyone to properly cleanse the teeth, and use only **KING BEE HONEY CREAM** to do it.

IT WHITENS THE TEETH,

IT GIVES HEALTH TO THE GUMS,

IT PERFUMES THE BREATH.

It is put up in the most convenient form possible, collapsible metal tubes, is very handy and economical for travelers.

PRICE, 25 CENTS PER TUBE.

FOR SALE BY ALL DRUGGISTS THROUGHOUT THE CIVILIZED WORLD.

KING BEE   **A RELIABLE**

TOOTHACHE   **REMEDY GUARANTEED**

GUM.   **TO GIVE RELIEF.**

FORMULA FROM THE POPULAR DENTAL SURGEON, DR. W. J. HURD,
St. Paul, formerly of Minneapolis.

We do not hesitate to recommend this article; retails for **10 Cts.** per bottle. For Sale by all Druggists.

Omelet.

Beat the yolks and whites of four eggs separately, add a teaspoon of flour, a little salt and pepper, and a cup of rich milk. Put a large piece of butter in a frying pan, pour in your mixture. It will at once begin to bubble. Slip a knife under it and raise once in a while to keep from burning. As soon as the eggs begin to set and hold together, fold over and shake the pan. Slide the omelet on a hot platter and serve at once. It will take from three to five minutes. A tablespoon of chopped parsley or a little grated onion can be added.

Bread Omelet.

Beat the yolks and whites of four eggs separately. Take two slices of bread moistened with sweet milk and rub it through a sieve, add the yolks and beat well; salt and pepper to taste. A little chopped parsley, ham and onion juice improves it. Bake as directed in the preceding recipe. Serve garnished with sprigs of parsley.

Corn Omelet.

Grate six ears of sweet corn, add three eggs, a little flour and a small cup of part cream and milk. Bake in an oven half an hour. Season well with salt, pepper and pieces of butter.

Scrambled Eggs.

Beat six eggs light. Put a large piece of butter in a pan and when hot stir in the eggs, stirring all the time. Cook about three minutes. Season with salt and pepper. Serve with toast garnished with slices of lemon; a little milk can be added to the beaten eggs.

Stuffed Eggs.

Boil six eggs hard. Remove the shells and cut the whites lengthwise. Remove the yolks, mash them, add a teaspoon of butter, a little onion juice and a little potted or devilled ham, and tongue or minced chicken; veal or lamb may be used. Season with pepper, salt and chopped parsley. Fill the whites with the mixture; press the halves together. Fry brown in hot fat or sprinkle crumbs over them and bake a delicate brown.

Devilled Eggs.

Cook six eggs twenty minutes. Remove the yolks and mash them with the back of a spoon to a smooth paste. Add a spoonful of butter, salt and a little cayenne pepper, a spoonful of vinegar and a quarter of a teaspoonful of mustard. Mix all together and press back into the whites. Set on a platter and garnish with slices of lemon and parsley.

THE GREAT REMEDY OF THE CENTURY.

SPENCERIAN BLOOD PURIFIER

Kidney and Liver Cure.

A PURE VEGETABLE MEDICINE.

Has been before the public for the past twenty years. Fifteen thousand bottles have been sold, giving satisfaction in every case.

Why pay out your money for trash medicines made in the East, said to have cured some one in Florida, got up to make money, when you can buy Spencerian Blood Purifier, Kidney and Liver Cure, made in this city, warranted to cure all diseases named on the label and bills, and recommended by the people of this city who have used it?

LIVER AND KIDNEY COMPLAINTS, Rheumatism, Catarrh, Scrofula, Erysipelas, Salt Rheum, Boils, Pimples, Sore Eyes, Costiveness, Diarrhœa, Dyspepsia, Sick Headache, Coughs. Malaria, Diabetis, Dropsy, Female Weakness, Impotency. Seminal Weakness, Frequen, Urination, Private Diseases, Piles, Grippe, Winter Cholerat etc. Price, $1.00 per Bottle; Six for $5.00.

The above named Diseases are warranted cured by the use of from two to twenty bottles of medicine. Try it and if not satisfied the money will be returned.

Sold by the Weinhold Drug Co., Price reduced to 2 bottles for $1.00.

Spencerian Lightning Pain Relief, for Diphtheria, Croup, Sore Throat, Toothache, Earache, Nervous and Sick Headache. Asthma, Catarrh, Chills, Cholera, Cricks, Cramps, Sprains, Rheumatism, Neuralgia, and all kinds of pain. Price, 25 cts.

The Weinhold Drug Co.,

Office: 239 First Ave. So.   MINNEAPOLIS, MINN.

FROSTING.

PARE off all the loose edges and if the cake is browned too much pare off some of the crust. Dust with a little flour. Always beat eggs to a stiff froth. Separate the whites from the yolks and place in the ice chest so they will cool and beat readily. Add your pulverized sugar gradually, and flavoring the last thing. In boiled frosting boil the sugar until it ropes or hairs from the spoon and turn hot upon the beaten eggs; beat until cold.

Boiled Frosting.

White of one egg, three-quarters of a cup of sugar, three tablespoons of hot water. Boil water and sugar and pour hot on the well beaten egg.

Chocolate Icing.

Make a boiled frosting of the whites of two eggs and two small cups of powdered sugar. Boil the sugar with four tablespoons of water. When all dissolved add one-quarter of a pound of scraped or grated chocolate Pour on the eggs and beat until cold. This will be enough for the filling. of a three-layer cake and for the top.

Yellow Frosting.

Yolk of an egg, powdered sugar to make a stiff icing. Flavor with vanilla or wine.

Hickory Nut Frosting.

Make a boiled frosting as given above and stir in one cup of chopped hickory nut meats and beat to a cream. Spread on the cake and smooth down with a knife dipped in cold water.

Frosting.

To the white of one egg beaten to a stiff froth add one cup of powdered sugar and a little lemon juice. Beat well, adding the sugar gradually. 1t

---

☞ ADVERTISERS are requested to read the recipe on page 32.

"I'VE more grit than you have," said the cake of chalk to the pound of sugar. "That's all right," replied the sugar, "but you haven't as much sand."—Truth.

Boiled Almond Frosting.

Whites of three eggs beaten to a stiff froth, one cup of granulated sugar dissolved in four tablespoons of hot water. Boil until it ropes from the spoon and pour over the eggs and beat until cold. Stir in one-half a pound of almonds pounded to a paste, and one-half teaspoon of vanilla. This will frost three cakes. 1u

This world is but a paradox.
And plainly does this show
In the fact that the surest "coming man"
Is the man with lots of go.
—Albany Times.

HAVE YOU ASTHMA OR BRONCHITIS?

Dr. R. Schiffmann, St. Paul, Minn., will mail a trial package of "Schiffmann's Asthma Cure" free to any sufferer. He advertises by giving it away. Never fails to give instant relief in worst cases and cures where others fail. Name this Cook Book and send address for a free trial package. Weinhold Drug Co. always keep a supply in stock.

☞ Your attention is respectfully called to page 32.

☞ Anything from a calling card to a large show card embossed in colors, or from a circular to a history of the world, can be produced by the Swinburne Printing Company, 9-11-13 Washington avenue north.

Young Mr. Dolley—Miss Amy, what is the best way of killing time in the winter? Amy—Sleigh it.—Truth.

☞ Caswell's Pectoral Balsam cures all coughs, colds and affections of the throat, chest and lungs.

Log Cabin Maple Syrup.

"The man or woman who hasn't written a poem on the subject of Christmas either has no poetic talent or is a person of extraordinary self-control."

☞ Caswell's Blood Cleaner will purify the blood.

☞ The Swinburne Printing Company would like to see you when you have any use for printer's ink.

As Far as the Surprise Went.

"And you really were surprised, Henry, dear?" said the young wife, gazing fondly into his eyes.
"Yes, indeed, dear," he replied with emphasis, as he gazed upon the pattern of the smoking-jacket; "I might even say startled."—Judge.

☞ Don't skip page 32, as it contains something of interest to you.

☞ Caswell's Pectoral Balsam is guaranteed to give satisfaction or money refunded.

"According to the familiar pictures of Santa Claus he is a most influential person, he has so much at the back of him."

☞ The only concern in the city making a specialty of high class printing, engraving and embossing is The Swinburne Printing Company.

☞ Gentlemen will find Chap-O-Lene very beneficial applied immediately after shaving.

☞ How to be happy, see page 32.

FRITTERS.

IN MAKING fritters, to make them light beat yolks and whites separately. Do not make too thick a batter; just thick enough to drop from a spoon easily. Use nice sweet lard or cottosuet, and have it at boiling heat. Test by dropping in a little of the batter; if it rises immediately and soon browns it is just right. In using fresh lard a good plan is to fry a few slices of potatoes in it before using. This clarifies it. Never use but a very little sugar in the batter, as sugar will make them heavy; sprinkle it over them when ready to serve.

Corn Fritters.

Add two eggs well beaten, to one pint of milk; mix well and add one can of fine corn. Add flour enough to make the batter the proper consistency and fry like griddle cakes. Serve these with chicken.

Corn Fritters.

Take one quart grated sweet corn, add two cups sweet milk, one cup of flour, a piece of butter two, eggs well beaten. Season with salt and pepper and fry like griddle cakes on a well greased griddle.

Oyster Fritters.

One pint of oysters, one pint of flour, a teaspoon of salt, half pint of water. Drain and chop oysters. Mix flour, oysters and salt together; add two well beaten eggs and a tablespoon of salad oil. Fry in boiling fat until brown. Butter can be used in place of salad oil.

Apple Fritters.

One cup of sweet milk, two cups of flour, heaping teaspoon of baking powder, two eggs, tablespoon of sugar, a little salt. Throw into the batter thin pieces of sour apples; about two. Fry to a light brown in hot lard and serve with maple syrup. These make a nice dessert.

☞THE cook will find something interesting on page 32.
☞Chap-O-Lene will positively cure chapped or rough skin.

74   THE WEINHOLD DRUG CO.

KICKAPOO INDIAN HERBAL REMEDIES

Kickapoo Indian Sagwa, Blood, Liver and Stomach Renovator, the greatest life giving blood cleansing and health restoring remedy known cures Dyspepsia, Liver Complaint, Malaria, Rheumatism, and all Stomach and Bowel Trouble. $1.00

KICKAPOO INDIAN WORM KILLER

For Worms in children; easily and safely removed in one night. Pin Worms, Stomach Worms and Round Worms. It physics the child and voids the worm every time. Easy to take. 25 Cents.

KICKAPOO INDIAN SALVE

Cures all kinds of Skin Diseases, Eruptions, Piles, Bruises, Itch, Ring Worms, Tetter, Scorbutic Eruptions, etc. Safe and easy remedy to use. 25 Cents.

KICKAPOO INDIAN COUGH CURE

Speedy relief and sure cure for Coughs, Colds, Asthma, Whooping Cough, Bronchitis, Hoarseness, loss of voice and all affections of Throat, Chest and Lungs. 50 Cts.

KICKAPOO INDIAN OIL

Quick cure for all kinds of pain; Neuralgia, Rheumatism, Toothache, soreness and pain in any part of the body, internal or external quickly removed. 25 Cents. These Indian Herbal Remedies are for sale by all Druggists in the U. S. at price marked on bottle.

HEALY & BIGELOW
NEW HAVEN, CONN.

Clam Fritters.

Use instead of oysters a pint of chopped clams, and the same batter as for oysters. Use more flour, as the liquor in the clams is apt to thin the batter.

Cream Fritters.

One pint of sweet milk, six eggs, two tablespoons of sugar, one cup of flour, three heaping tablespoons of butter, salt spoon of salt. Flavor with a little nutmeg, lemon or orange. Put ingredients together and cook in a double boiler. Butter a cake pan and pour in the mixture; cool and cut into small squares. Dip the squares in beaten egg and crumbs and fry in hot lard, or do not cook mixture but drop by spoonfuls in boiling fat.

Banana Fritters.

One cup of flour, yolks of two eggs, a pinch of salt, two tablespoons of melted butter or lard, enough water or milk to make a batter. Add the whites beaten stiff, and stir in three or four bananas cut in slices. Drop the batter by spoonfuls in boiling lard. Do not crowd. If the fat is hot they will take from three to five minutes. Serve with cream sauce or maple syrup.

Lemon Fritters.

Three eggs, a pint of flour, one-half tea cup of sugar, a gill of milk, juice and grated peel of one lemon. Serve with maple syrup or a foaming sauce.

Hasty Fritters.

Put three heaping tablespoons of flour into a bowl, and enough boiling water on it to make a stiff paste, stirring and beating well to prevent it from becoming lumpy. Let it cool and stir into it the yolks of three eggs and whites of two. Beat well together and drop by spoonfuls in boiling lard and fry a delicate brown. Serve on a dish with a spoonful of preserves, marmalade or jelly.

Peach Fritters.

Make a batter of a cup of sweet milk, a pint and a half of flour and a half cup of yeast. Set in a warm place to rise. When very light add two well beaten eggs, two tablespoons of sugar, a large piece of butter and a pinch of salt. Knead with the hands into a loaf. Pinch off pieces of the dough, and in the centre of each piece put a stoned peach. Roll up in the dough and put in a buttered pan some distance apart, to rise again. Fry in hot fat, and serve with any kind of sauce. Use apricots or canned peaches in the same way.

1w

D. RANSOM, SON & CO.'S
Standard Family Medicines.

Trask's Magnetic Ointment,
   For all Inflammations.

Ransom's Hive Syrup and Tolu,
   For Coughs, Croup, Etc.

Miller's Magnetic Balm,
   For Colic, Summer Complaints, Colds, Etc

Anderson's Dermador,
   A Liniment for Man and Beast.

King of the Blood,
   A Blood Purifier.

Halbert's Star Remedy,
   For all Kidney, Liver and Stomach Troubles..

Retail Trade Supplied by Jobbers who will Quote Prices.

D. Ransom, Son & Co., Proprietors,
BUFFALO, N. Y., U. S. A.

FISH.

FISH is considered a very reliable article of food. It is not so nutritious and stimulating as meat, but very wholesome. It is especially adapted to people upon whom there are great demands for nervous energy. It is so easily digested and contains so little fat and is richer in phosphorus than meat. Fish, to be eatable, must be perfectly fresh. Good fish will have a firm, hard meat. If it looks pale and limp reject it as unfit to cook. Fish should be cleaned as soon as caught. Remove the scales with a sharp knife and cut off the head and tail. Wash in cold salted water thoroughly, and wipe dry, then place on the ice until ready to cook. Do not soak fresh fish. Always cook fish very well done. We have the salt water, fresh water and shell fish. Pieces of cold fish left over make very nice salads and croquettes. Large fish are usually boiled and the small ones fried. Oily fish, as mackerel, salmon, blue fish, should never be fried.

Baked Fish.

Prepare a fish as given above; rub the fish inside and out with salt and pepper. Fill with a dressing made of bread crumbs. Sew it up and put in a hot pan with beef drippings and a piece of butter. Sprinkle over it a little flour. Bake an hour. This is especially nice for white fish. The dressing can be left out. Lay pieces of salt pork on top of the fish.

Baked Trout.

Clean well and wipe dry. Lay on a rack in a roasting pan. Bake slowly, basting with butter and water. When done serve with a white sauce poured around it.

Boiled Fish.

To make boiled fish palatable, serve always with a rich sauce. Put the fish in hot water with a teaspoonful of salt. Cook thirty minutes. Put the fish in a piece of strong white cotton cloth if you have no fish kettle. This keeps it in shape. Put a tablespoon of vinegar in the water in which the fish is boiled.

☞ THE place to get high class printing is at 9-11-13 Washington avenue north.

Gold Dust Flour

....MADE BY THE....

HOLLY FLOURING MILLS,

IS EQUAL TO THE BEST PATENT.

The "HOLLY" has been in Successful Operation in Minneapolis for Twenty Years.

Highest Award at the World's Fair.

IMPORTANT NOTICE.

If your grocer WILL NOT sell you GOLD DUST, send down to the mill after it yourself, and we will give you ONE SACK or TWENTY, at WHOLESALE PRICE.

C. McC. REEVE,

President.

Baked Fish With Oyster Stuffing.

Remove the head, tail and skin. Rub with salt and lemon juice. Make a dressing as follows: One pint of oysters, one cup of seasoned and buttered cracker or bread crumbs. Drain oysters and roll in the crumbs. Fill the fish and sprinkle the crumbs over it. Bake in the oven over a little water in a roasting pan forty minutes. Serve with tomato either poured around it or in side dishes.

Fried Fish.

All small fish like brook trout, smelts, etc., are best fried. Salt them well after they are cleaned and dried, and roll in Indian meal or flour. Fry half a pound of salt pork a crisp brown. Take the pork from the pan and put in the fish. Fry brown on one side and turn and fry brown on the other. Flour can be used in place of Indian meal.

Salt Codfish.

The fish should be washed and soaked in several waters. Put on in cold water, and as soon as it comes to a boil put on the back of the stove, and keep it hot; but do not let it boil. Pour off the water and pour on a cream sauce, or serve the fish with drawn butter.

Fish Balls.

Prepare codfish as above. Take mashed potatoes left from dinner; season well with butter, pepper and salt. A beaten egg makes them lighter. Mix thoroughly with the codfish. Form with the hands into flat cakes and fry brown in hot lard or drippings.

Canned Salmon.

This is nice served with a warm cream sauce, or heat a cup of milk, add a large piece of butter, pepper and salt. Pour over the fish and let it stand in a hot oven for a few minutes. Serve hot. Salt mackerel is nice served this way.

Turbot.

Cook a white fish tender. Remove the bones. Season with pepper and salt. Take one pint of milk and thicken with two tablespoons of flour. When cool add two eggs, two tablespoons of butter and a little chopped onion and parsley. Put in a baking dish a layer of crumbs, then a layer of fish. Cover the top with crumbs and pour over all the sauce. Bake half an hour. A grating of cheese makes it nice. Use haddock in place of white fish.

1y

☞ WEDDING Invitations, Announcements, At Home, etc. High class work produced by The Swinburne Printing Company, 9-11-13 Washington avenue north.

VAL. BLATZ BREWING CO.

MILWAUKEE, WIS.

Minneapolis Branch,  1314 - 1316 - 1318 South Sixth St.

 TELEPHONE 206.

FINE TABLE BEER

OUR BRANDS ARE:

TIVOLI, WIENER, IMPERIAL, PRIVATE STOCK, MUENCHENER.

Family Trade Solicited.

Orders Delivered to any part of the City.

SHELL FISH.

Clam Stew.

Take half a peck of clams, wash the shells. Put in a kettle with a cup of water. Cook until the shells open. Take out of the shells, strain the juice and let the clams come to a boil. Add one pint of milk, a large piece of butter, pepper and salt and a few small crackers rolled fine. To fry them take them from the shells and dry them, roll in beaten egg and cracker crumbs and fry in hot lard.

Crabs.

Remove from the shells the same as clams. Dip in beaten egg and cracker crumbs and fry brown. Serve with tartar sauce.

Lobster.

The lobster should be perfectly fresh. Never cook it too long, for long cooking makes it tough. Prepare the lobster as given in the miscellaneous recipes. Lobster can be broiled by covering it with soft butter, and dredge it with flour. Place on a broiler and cook a delicate brown.

Stewed Lobster.

Take the meat of a lobster and cut it into small pieces. Put two tablespoons of butter, two of flour, two cups of water or stock, pepper and salt. Add the lobster, cook ten minutes and serve. This mixture, when cold, can be cut up into chops and dipped in beaten egg and crumbs and fried in boiling fat. Garnish with parsley and slices of lemon.

Oysters on the Half Shell.

Do not open until ready to serve. Place six oysters on each plate in half the shell and a piece of lemon placed in the centre of the plate.

Raw Oysters on Ice.

Take a block of ice and make a hole in the top by putting on a very hot flatiron. Pour off the water and repeat this until there is quite a cavity. Season the oysters with salt, pepper and vinegar. Put in a cool place. Pour the oysters in the cavity and cover with pieces of lemon. Cover the oysters with parsley or some bright flowers.

Caswell's Beef, Wine and Iron is the Ideal Tonic.

Scalloped Oysters.

One pint of oysters. Butter a dish. Put in a layer of crumbs, butter, pepper and salt and a layer of oysters and so on until the dish is full, finishing with a layer of crumbs. Moisten with milk or water. Bake until brown. Use the liquor also for wetting. A cup of cream is an addition. Some add lemon juice, wine or Worcestershire sauce. Oysters are nice escalloped in shells. Prepare the same as above and serve in shells.

Fried Oysters.

Drain carefully and pick out all the bits of shell, season with salt and pepper. Roll in beaten egg, then in cracker crumbs and drop singly into hot fat. Skim out and serve with cold slaw or slices of lemon. Some use Indian meal in place of cracker crumbs. First roll in the meal, then in the egg and again in the meal.

Creamed Oysters.

Parboil the oysters until plump. Make a cream sauce and season with cayenne and celery salt. Pour over the oysters. Serve on slices of toast.

Panned Oysters.

Take large oysters—about a dozen large ones. Put on the oysters in their liquor; add a tablespoon of butter, a little lemon juice, a tablespoon of fine cracker crumbs. Season with salt and pepper and a little cayenne. Cook one minute and place on slices of nice buttered toast.

Broiled Oysters.

Take large oysters, drain and dry them. Season with pepper and salt, and broil on a wire broiler or place on a rack under the blaze in the oven of a gas range and turn when brown. Dip in butter and then in powdered crumbs and broil.

Oyster Patties.

Take oysters and put in a pan with their liquor. Add a cup of milk, a little lemon rind, a large piece of butter, pepper and salt. Stir into the milk a teaspoon of flour; stir and let the mixture simmer for a few minutes. Line patty pans with puff paste. Fill while hot with the oysters.

2a

☛ EVERY business man can profit if he will carefully follow the recipe on page 32.

"As much money is spent on funerals as ef a man's social standing in de next wurld depended on de size ob his funeral-bill in dis."
Log Cabin Maple Syrup.

Pigs in Blankets.

Season oysters with salt and pepper. Cut thin slices of bacon, wrap an oyster in each slice and fasten with a tooth pick. Put in a frying pan and cook long enough to cook the bacon. Put on slices of toast just as they are.

Oyster Pie.

Line a deep pudding dish with a nice rich crust. Dredge the crust with flour, pour in a pint of oysters, season with salt and pepper and bits of butter. Sprinkle with flour and cover with a top crust. Make an opening in the top. 2b

☞ How to make Us happy, read the recipe on page 32 and follow it.

☞ Caswell's Pectoral Balsam is a perfect cough cure.

What's in a Name?

"No," said the fair young maid, as she listened to congratulations tinctured with malice, envy and all uncharitableness; "Guggenheimer is neither a beautiful nor a distinguished name. But when it goes with one of the largest ready-made pants businesses on West Broadway, it's a very reasonably decent sort of a Christmas present; and I want you to understand that I've got it."

☞ High class printing and engraving. The Swinburne Printing Company.

HAVE YOU ASTHMA OR BRONCHITIS?

Dr. R. Shiffmann, St. Paul, Minn., will mail a trial package of "Schiffmann's Asthma Cure" free to any sufferes. He advertises by giving it away. Never fails to give instant relief in worst cases and cures where others fail. Name this Cook Book and send address for a free trial package. Weinhold Drug Co. always keep a supply in stock.

"The old liberty bell has gone home. Chicago has found it exactly what it was cracked up to be."

☞ Child's Cough Cure is prepared especially for children.

☞ We guarantee our work. If it is not entirely satisfactory send it back; don't use it up and then ask for a rebate, as you won't get it. We don't care to deal with cranks. The Swinburne Printing Company.

Dudes are now using chrysanthemums in connection with their overcoats, to keep themselves warm.

☞ High class printing, engraving and embossing at 9-11-13 Washington avenue north.

☞ If you are going to be married read page 32.

A Master of Fiction.

Applicant—I understand you have a place for a writer of pure fiction.
Publisher—I have. Are you one?
"I think so."
"What have you done in that line?"
"Written several books for railroads, descriptive of the attractions of their summer resort regions, and—"
"That is sufficient! You may go to work at once."

☞ The housekeeper should not fail to study page 32.

STANDARD PREPARATIONS.

MRS. WINSLOW'S SOOTHING SYRUP

Has been used for over FIFTY YEARS by MILLIONS of MOTHERS for their CHILDREN WHILE TEETHING, with PERFECT SUCCESS. It SOOTHS the CHILD, SOFTENS the GUMS, ALLAYS all PAIN; CURES WIND COLIC, and is the best remedy for DIARRHŒA. Sold by Druggists in every part of the world. Be sure and ask for "Mrs. Winslow's Soothing Syrup," and take no other kind. **Retail price, 25 cents a bottle.**

THE ANGLO-AMERICAN DRUG CO., Proprietors,
217 Fulton Street, NEW YORK, N. Y.

BROWN'S BRONCHIAL TROCHES.

An Old and World-Renowned Remedy for the Relief and Cure of Coughs, Hoarsness, and all Throat Troubles. Indispensable to Speakers and Singers.

For over forty years they have been recommended by physicians, and widely used, being known all over the world as one of the few staple cough remedies. **Sold only in boxes. Retail price, 25 cents, 50 cents, $1.00.**

JOHN I. BROWN & SONS, Proprietors,
184 Summer Street, BOSTON, MASS.

BROWN'S VERMIFUGE COMFITS OR WORM LOZENGERS.

This valuable combination, although effectual in destroying worms, can do no possible injury to the most delicate child. Successfully used by physicians, and found to be absolutely sure in eradicating Worms. Much sickness, undoubtedly, with children, attributed to other causes, is occasioned by **Worms. Retail price, 25 cents a box.**

THE CURTIS & BROWN M'F'G CO., L'd, Proprietors,
217 Fulton Street, NEW YORK, N. Y.

BROWN'S HOUSEHOLD PANACEA.

Unequalled for relieving pain. Taken internally, it gives prompt and effective relief in all cases of Cramps, Summer Complaints, Chills, and Pain in the Side, Stomach or Bowels. Its effectiveness is increased by simultaneous external application on flannel or by rubbing.

Used externally for healing and removing soreness from Bruises, Cuts and Burns, and relieving Toothache, Sprains, Stiff Joints and Rheumatic Affections, it produces excellent results.

Stronger than any similar preparation, and invaluable as a household remedy for speedily relieving aches and pains. **Retail price, 25 cents a bottle.**

THE CURTIS & BROWN M'F'G CO., L'd, Proprietors,
217 Fulton Street, NEW YORK, N. Y.

BROWN'S CAMPHORATED SAPONACEOUS DENTIFRICE.

A Superior Preparation and a most Agreeable Article for Cleansing and Preserving the Teeth and Purifying the Breath.

Microscopical examination by Dr. H. I. BOWDITCH of the matter deposited on the teeth, have proved that those only who use Soap as a dentifrice were free from the accumulation of animal and vegetable parasites upon the teeth and gums. The addition of camphor strengthens and relieves soreness of the gums and teeth, and maintains them constantly in a healthy state. **Retail price, 25 cents a jar.**

Prepared by JOHN I. BROWN & SONS,
THE CURTIS & BROWN M'F'G CO., L'd, Proprietors,
217 Fulton Street, NEW YORK, N. Y.

And the Celebrated "DONTINA" Powder for the teeth. **25 cents a jar.**

ALL FOR SALE BY

WEINHOLD DRUG CO.   MINNEAPOLIS. MINNESOTA.

MEAT.

MEAT is a term given to the muscular flesh, heart, liver, brains, tongue and fat of animals. We have three classes—meat, poultry and game. Meat should always be cooked in such a way as to retain the largest proportion of juice. To boil fresh meat to retain the juice, put into boiling water and boil rapidly for fifteen minutes, then let it simmer slowly until done. Salt sets the juices free. When meat is boiled for stock, use cold water to extract all the juice and nutriment in the meat. Boil meat always slowly and keep covered closely. Salt meat should be put on in cold water and the water changed several times according to the saltness of it. In roasting meats baste frequently, and turn; to roast them evenly the new roasting pans with racks do the work with very little care. Have the oven very hot when the meat is first put in and after twenty minutes lower and keep a regular fire. The time of roasting depends on the size of the roast. Allow for rare meats fifteen minutes to the pound and twenty for roasts well done. Broiling is the most wholesome way of cooking steaks, chops, ham, etc. Frying in fat renders the meat not nearly so digestible. We use meat all seasons of the year, but certain kinds are better at certain seasons. Beef at all times, and is the staple meat. Pork is good in fall and winter, veal in the spring, lamb in the summer and poultry and game in the fall and winter. Good beef has a firm flesh and should be a bright red, the fat dry and crumble easily. It is much better some time after it is killed; at least a week old. Mutton and lamb are best kept for some time before cooking. In veal the fat should be white and the flesh pink or flesh color. If it is white the blood has been taken out of the calf before it has been killed, and it is unfit to eat. Veal to be palatable should be highly seasoned and cooked very well done. Pork is the hardest meat to digest and should never be eaten by children or people with weak stomachs. It is very important to cook pork thoroughly and very well done. The meat of poultry is excellent for invalids, as it abounds in phosphorus. All game has a strong odor. It should be kept until tender, but no longer. All poultry and game should be

"Dr. Scott's Electric"

goods are world-renowned for the beneficent power of Electro-Magnetism they contain, and popular because this curative agent is combined in articles of every day use.

Electric Corsets cure Weak Back, Indigestion, Spinal Trouble, Rheumatism. Price, $1.00, $1.25, $1.50, $2.00 and $3.00.

Electric Hair Brushes for Falling Hair, Baldness, Dandruff, and Diseases of the Scalp. Price, $1.00, $1.50, $2.00, $2.50 and $3.00.

Electric Belts cure Rheumatism, Nervous Debility, Indigestion, Backache, Liver and Kidney Trouble. Price, $3.00, $5.00 and $10.00.

Electric Safety Razor, a safeguard against Barber's Itch, Pimples, and Blotches; perfect security from cutting the face when shaving. A novice can use it. Price, $2.00.

Electric Plasters, Insoles, Flesh Brushes, Tooth Brushes, Curlers, and Appliances.

A full stock of our goods can be found at WEINHOLD DRUG Co., Minneapolis, Minn. Our book, "The Doctor's Story," giving full information concerning all our goods, free on application. ADDRESS

GEO. A. SCOTT,
842 Broadway,   -   -   NEW YORK.

Agents Wanted.   Mention this Book.

cleaned and drawn as soon as they are killed. In choosing chickens and turkeys choose those which have short, plump legs and yellow feet, and the breasts firm and plump. Feel of the cartilage at the end of the breast bone; if it is soft the fowl is young and tender, if hard and not pliable it is old and tough.

Roast Beef.

Wipe the meat with a clean towel, dredge the sides and top with flour, pepper and salt. Place on a rack in a roasting pan and put in a very hot oven; have the pan hot. Cover closely and allow for rare beef fifteen minutes to a pound. If the meat is roasted in a common dripping pan put in a little water and baste occasionally. Uncover your pan a few minutes before the meat is done to brown nicely. Flour and salt together forms a paste which retains the juices of the meat. Yorkshire pudding is nice baked and served with roast beef. (Look in the recipes for Yorkshire pudding.)

Broiled Beefsteak.

Lay a thick, tender beefsteak on a gridiron with a little beef suet over a bed of hot coals or place the rack under the blaze of a gas range. When done on one side, turn quickly and cook the other. Put on a hot platter, season with pepper, salt and bits of butter.

Beefsteak and Onions.

Slice the onions thin. Put the steak in a hot pan, cover with the onions and season with salt and pepper. Cover tightly. When the meat has been browned on one side remove the onions, turn the steak, replace them and cook until done.

Beef Loaf.

Three pounds of beef chopped fine, one-half a pound of salt pork chopped fine; mix with three well beaten eggs, six crackers rolled fine, one tablespoon of salt, teaspoon of pepper and sage and thyme to taste. Put bits of butter and a little water in a pan and bake an hour and a quarter. Baste occasionally. Slice when served. Veal can be used in the place of beef.

Beef Tongue.

Wash a fresh tongue; cook in boiling salted water with a small pod of red pepper in it; boil until it can be easily pierced with a fork; remove the skin and set in a cool place. Serve sliced cold for lunch, or serve in a jelly. 2d

---

"SILENCE is the safest course for any man to adopt who distrusts himself."

Washburn-Crosby Co.'s "Best"

FLOUR

IS THE

Leading Bread Flour of Minnesota.

50,000 BARRELS
Sold Annually to Minneapolis Trade.

YOUR GROCER KEEPS IT.

ONCE USED.

ALWAYS USED.

Pot Roast.

Take a good piece from the rump or round, with some fat in it. Put in a kettle with as little water as will cover it. Cover closely, and as the water boils away add more. When the meat is tender the water will be all boiled away. The fat will brown it. If there is not enough add some drippings or a piece of butter. Brown over a slow fire. Make a gravy of the browned drippings.

Beef a'la Mode.

Take six pounds of good round beef. Trim off rough edges. Cut half a pound of salt pork into strips half an inch thick. Soak the beef in one cup of boiling vinegar in which has been thrown one onion chopped fine, two teaspoons of salt, half a teaspoonful of mustard, pepper, cloves and allspice. Let the meat stand in this. Pierce the beef with a sharp knife with holes an inch apart. Place in these holes the strips of pork. Put a cloth around the meat and pin it securely. Dredge with flour. Put chopped onion, carrot and half a turnip in hot fat, and fry until brown. Brown the meat in the fat and the vegetables. Put in some water and simmer four hours. Garnish with potato balls and small onions.

Hamberg Steak.

Take a round steak and pound it well. Fry two or three onions brown, in butter; spread the onions on the steak and fold it; season with salt, pepper and butter, and fry brown. A round steak can be chopped fine and mixed with the fried onions, and seasoned well. Mold into flat cakes and fry well done.

Corned Beef.

Soak in cold water for an hour if very salt. Put in cold water, and if still salt change the water. Simmer slowly for several hours. This is nice with a boiled dinner.

Fried Liver.

Soak ten minutes in boiling water to draw out the blood; drain and remove the thin skin; cut into pieces; cut nice slices of bacon, fry crisp, but not brown; take out and fry the liver in the bacon fat. This can be served with the slices of bacon and a brown gravy seasoned with onion and lemon juice. Season with salt and pepper.

So far as getting Christmas presents is concerned it's like a lottery—you have to take your chances.

☞ Are you going to lay this book down and not read that recipe on page 32.

Few love to hear the sins they love to act.—Shakespeare.

GESSLER'S
MAGIC
HEADACHE
WAFERS

THE KIND THAT CURE.

From a Doctor.

Mr. Max Gessler:

Dear Sir—I have used your "Magic Headache Wafers" in my daily practice and find them to give excellent satisfaction. I have prescribed them in a great number of cases and have yet to hear from the first case that your "Wafers" failed to cure. I do not hesitate to recommend them (without solicitation) to both "practitioners and the public" as a "sure cure." Yours very truly,

DR. J. T. FELLING,
Des Moines, Ia.

From a Chemist.

I have personally made an analysis of Gessler's Magic Headache Wafers and find them free from quinine, morphine, opium and all narcotic or harmful alkaloids; they are perfectly safe and I can cheerfully recommend them for headache and neuralgia.

ANDREW S. MITCHELL,
Analytical Chemist,
Milwaukee, Wis.

$100.00 REWARD

To any Chemist that will find a trace of Opium, Morphine, Chloral, Quinine or any harmful alkaloid in **Gessler's Magic Headache Wafers.**

Druggists the world over guarantee Gessler's Magic Headache Wafers to cure or will refund money.

MANUFACTURED BY

MAX GESSLER, PH. C.,
MILWAUKEE, WIS.

Tripe.

Drain, dredge with flour and broil on a gridiron; season with salt, pepper and butter, or dip in a batter made of egg and cracker crumbs, and fry in hot lard.

Lamb Chops.

Trim and broil over hot fire; season with salt and pepper, and serve with green peas. Wrap the end of the bone of each cutlet in fringed tissue paper and lay them overlapping one another on the platter.

Roast Lamb.

Prepare and roast the same as roast beef. Lamb is better roasted longer than beef. Serve with mint sauce.

Roast Veal.

Remove the bone and fill the cavity with highly seasoned and moist dressing; dredge with salt, pepper and flour; put strips of salt pork or bacon on top, and bake half an hour for each pound. Serve with horse-radish sauce.

Breaded Veal.

Take slices of veal from the leg; remove all bone and skin; season with salt and pepper; roll in beaten egg, then in fine cracker or bread crumbs. Fry out several pieces of salt pork and fry the cutlets brown in the fat. Garnish with slices of lemon and parsley. Make a gravy with the fat left in the pan and two tablespoons of flour and a cup of water.

Sweet-Breads.

Those found in veal are the best. They are two glands lying along the back and in the breast. Put them in cold water; remove the membranes; cook in salted water with a tablespoon of lemon juice; put in cold water; roll in fine bread crumbs and beaten egg, and fry in hot fat. Fry with a slice of bacon fastened to each side. They can be served with cream sauce. Sweet-breads are also prepared by dipping them in a batter made of one cup of milk, one egg, one cup of flour, a pinch of salt and a little baking powder; fry in salt pork fat.

Roast Pork.

The loin or spareribs are the best for roasting. Rub with pepper, salt and flour and bake thirty minutes for each pound. Rub with a little sage and thyme. Bake well done.

THE little ones make so much noise on Christmas because they've been taught that it is a holler-day.

THE WEINHOLD DRUG CO.

Why Drink
Impure River Water?

Fountain Spring Water

Delivered Daily

At Reasonable Rates.

We aim

to have the

BEST GRADES of

Coal, Coke,

and Wood.

Patrons of the
THEATRES
Furnished with
Fountain Spring Water.

Prompt Delivery.

Telephone 1465.

Ham.

Ham is best broiled over a quick fire on a gridiron. Serve with dropped or poached eggs. If the ham is very salt freshen it with a little cold water and bring it to the boiling point.

Boiled Ham.

Pour boiling water over it and let it stand until cold. Put in a large kettle and boil five hours. Pull off the skin. Put in an oven awhile. This brings out a great quantity of fat. Serve the nicest part in slices cold. Save the bits for sandwiches and omelets.

POULTRY AND GAME.

Baked Chicken.

Clean thoroughly. Use for a filling a pint of dry, fine bread crumbs. Either grate, or pound the stale bread in a bag; add half a cup of milk, half a cup of butter and the yolk of an egg. Season with a teaspoon of salt, half a teaspoonful of powdered sage and summer savory, a teaspoon of chopped parsley and pepper. Fill the chicken and sew up. Baste in the oven every ten or fifteen minutes with a little water and butter, or dredge with salt and rub a little butter over the chicken and dredge with flour. This keeps in the juices.

Fried Chicken.

Cut up a chicken by cutting through the loose skin between the legs and body; bend the legs over and cut at the joint. Then cut off the wings. Make an incision in the skin near the vent and cut the membrane lying between the breastbone and the tail down the backbone on each side. Now you can easily remove the gizzard, liver, heart and intestines. Remove the crop carefully. Fry the back, thighs, legs and wings in hot fat or drippings from salt pork or bacon. After these have fried awhile put in the breast. Season with chopped onion, herbs, and salt and pepper. Turn when browned and done on one side and brown on the other. This is only nice for very young, tender fowls. When the chicken is older and larger steam, or cook tender, and then fry as directed. Serve with the heart and liver fried brown. Garnish with fried oysters or rice croquettes.

THERE is usually a great big difference between the property-man and the man of property.—Brooklyn Eagle.

Crescent Creamery Butter.

The keynote of a SUCCESSFUL DINNER is good butter. After an experience of fifteen years in manufacturing the finest grades of butter for the best classes of trade everywhere, we feel confident that we are now master of the art. Our butter is always uniform in quality and is made by the latest improved

SEPARATOR PROCESS.

Our motto is CLEANLINESS. Our prices are reasonable, and our goods are guaranteed. In buying butter be sure to ask for the "CRESCENT" or "NORTHFIELD" brands of butter and get perfect satisfaction.

SOLD BY ALL THE LEADING GROCERS
AND BUTTER DEALERS
OF MINNEAPOLIS AND ST. PAUL.

The Crescent Creamery Co.,
MINNEAPOLIS.

Telephone 610.

Chicken Fricassee.

Cut the chicken up as directed. Put in boiling water and add a little salt and pepper. Cook an hour and a half or less time according to the age of the chicken. Remove the bones. Dredge the meat with flour, salt and pepper and brown in hot butter or fry out a few slices of salt pork and use the fat to brown the chicken. Strain the liquor, add the fat left in the pan, one cup of cream or milk, a large tablespoon of butter and two of flour and the last thing a well beaten egg. Put a sliced onion in the water in which the chicken was boiled.

Chicken Stew.

Prepare the chicken as above, and instead of frying, add a tablespoon of butter, a tablespoon of flour and season with pepper and salt. Dumplings can be added if desired. Serve with the gravy poured around the chicken and surround with the dumplings. A few tomatoes cut up and a sliced onion with parsley, cayenne and black pepper makes a palatable stew.

Chicken Pie.

Prepare the chicken as for a stew and season the same. Put in a deep dish with a bottom and top crust and bake. Make a rich baking powder or sour milk crust and cut incisions in the top to let out the steam. A few sliced potatoes, a sliced onion, a little chopped parsley and celery improves the pie greatly. Some use only the top crust and it is a better plan to do so.

Roast Turkey.

Prepare the turkey by singeing the hairs. Remove the pin feathers with a knife. Cut the head off, remove the wind pipe and crop. Remove the internal organs and wash inside and out thoroughly. Fill with a dressing and sew up. Put the turkey on the rack in the pan, rub well with soft butter and dredge with flour, pepper aud salt. Baste often and when half the time is up, turn. Allow three hours for an eight-pound turkey. Serve with cranberry sauce. Use oystee dressing in place of the dressing given. Dressing: Take one pint of fine bread crumbs. Season highly with powdered herbs, pepper and salt. Moisten with half a cup of butter and milk to make it quite moist. Add one well beaten egg. (See "Miscellaneous" for oyster dressing.)

CUSTOMER (in cheap restaurant)—"Let me have some ham and cabbage." Waiter (shouting to cook)—"One actor with a chrysanthemum."

☛ You are invited to call or write for samples of work when in need of anything in the line of high class printing, from a calling card to a three-sheet poster.—The Swinburne Printing Company, 9-11-13 Washington Avenue North.

Chicken Curry.

Cut up the chicken and remove the bones. Season with salt and pepper, and brown in hot butter. Fry a large onion cut in slices in the butter left, add a tablespoon of flour, teaspoon of sugar and a teaspoonful of curry powder. Brown in the butter; add one cup of water or stock, a cup of strained tomatoes, and salt and pepper to taste. Pour this on the chicken and cook an hour longer. Serve with a border of boiled rice. Use veal and lamb in the same way.

Scalloped Turkey.

Take bits of turkey left from dinner, butter a pan, sprinkle in a layer of crumbs, then a layer of chopped cold turkey. Season with salt and pepper; add another layer of crumbs and so on until the pan is full. Moisten well with milk. Add bits of dressing and gravy left over. This is better than all milk. Bake brown. Cold turkey minced makes very nice croquettes and omelets.

Roast Ducks.

Pick, singe and dress the same as a turkey. Tie the wings and legs securely and stuff with a pint of bread crumbs, three ounces of butter, (bits of salt pork are nice) two chopped onions, teaspoon of mixed powdered herbs, and salt and pepper to taste. Do not stuff very full and stitch the opening firmly together to keep the fat out. Place in a roasting pan and baste occasionally with salt and water. Turn often and bake for a full hour; if very young thirty minutes. Some always parboil a duck or goose before roasting. It is a good plan, for it disposes of some of the surplus fat. A dressing of equal parts of mashed potatoes and onions, seasoned well, can be used if preferred.

Rabbits.

Skin and prepare as in fricasseed chicken or chicken stew. Serve with a white sauce the same as with chicken. To make a pie of them follow the directions for chicken pie.

HAVE YOU ASTHMA OR BRONCHITIS?

Dr. R. Schiffmann, St. Paul, Minn., will mail a trial package of "Schiffmann's Asthma Cure" free to any sufferer. He advertises by giving it away. Never fails to give instatnt relief in worst cases and cures where others fail. Name this Cook Book and send address for a free trial package. Weinhold Drug Co. always keep a supply in stock.

No ashes are lighter than those of incense, and few things burn out sooner.
—Lander.

Quail on Toast.

Pick them and singe them with paper; cut off heads and legs. Soak in salt and water with a little soda added. Dry well, lard them with bacon. That is, cut salt pork in narrow, thin strips and run the strips with a larding needle under the skin of the bird; leave the ends exposed. Rub salt on them and place on a broiler and cook half an hour. Serve on slices of buttered toast. All game should be rare.

Venison.

Venison may be cooked the same as mutton or beef. It should be cooked rare and served with cranberry or currant jelly. Venison steaks should be broiled the same as beefsteaks.

☞ You are invited to call or write for samples of work when in need of anything in the line of high class printing, from a calling card to a three-sheet poster.—The Swinburne Printing Company, 9-11-13 Washington Avenue North.

HAVE YOU ASTHMA OR BRONCHITIS?

Dr. R. Shiffmann, St. Paul, Minn., will mail a trial package of "Schiffmann's Asthma Cure" free to any sufferes. He advertises by giving it away. Never fails to give instant relief in worst cases and cures where others fail. Name this Cook Book and send address for a free trial package. Weinhold Drug Co. always keep a supply in stock.

☞ WE guarantee our work. If it is not entirely satisfactory send it back; don't use it up and then ask for a rebate, as you won't get it. We don't care to deal with cranks. The Swinburne Printing Company.

☞ Child's Cough Cure is prepared especially for children.

☞ HIGH class printing, engraving and embossing at 9-11-13 Washington avenue north.

☞ IF you are going to be married read page 32.

"SILENCE is the safest course for any man to adopt who distrusts himself."

☞ ANYTHING from a calling card to a large show card embossed in colors, or from a circular to a history of the world, can be produced by the Swinburne Printing Company, 9-11-13 Washington avenue north.

☞ Caswell's Pectoral Balsam cures all coughs, colds and affections of the throat, chest and lungs.

☞ THE only concern in the city making a specialty of high class printing, engraving and embossing is The Swinburne Printing Company.

☞ Caswell's Pectoral Balsam is guaranteed to give satisfaction or money refunded.

☞ DON'T skip page 32, as it contains something of interest to you.

☞ Gentlemen will find Chap-O-Lene very beneficial applied immediately after shaving.

GRAVIES.

Gravy for Roast Turkey.

Put the giblets, liver, gizzard and heart on to boil; boil until very tender. Chop fine. Pour off the fat from the roasting pan and pour the settlings into a sauce pan. Take a few tablespoons of the fat and put in two tablespoons of flour; add to the liquor and put in the chopped meat; season with pepper and salt and strain. Brown the flour before adding it to the fat.

Gravy for Roast Beef.

When the meat is done remove from the pan and put on the platter and put in the oven. Let the liquid in the pan settle, pour off the fat. Pour in a pint of water or stock. Put a few tablespoons of the hot fat in a sauce pan and add two tablespoons of browned flour; add the hot liquid, season with salt and pepper and stir until it thickens. Strain and serve with the meat.

Chicken Gravy.

Boil the giblets and chop them. Put the water in which they were boiled in the pan from which the baked chicken has been taken; add half a pint of chicken stock or water and thicken with two tablespoons of flour. Stir in half a cup of cream and season with salt and pepper. Strain and serve with baked chicken. If there is not fat enough in the chicken add a piece of butter. 2k

---

HAVE YOU ASTHMA OR BRONCHITIS?

Dr. R. Schiffmann, St. Paul, Minn., will mail a trial package of "Schiffmann's Asthma Cure" free to any sufferer. He advertises by giving it away. Never fails to give instant relief in worst cases and cures where others fail. Name this Cook Book and send address for a free trial package. Weinhold Drug Co. always keep a supply in stock.

☞ How to be happy, see page 32.

MISCELLANEOUS RECIPES.

Lettuce Sandwiches.

Spread thin slices of bread, trimmed and shaped, with seasoned Mayonnaise dressing. Put between the slices a small, crisp lettuce leaf and serve for lunch or tea.

Egg Sandwiches.

Cut bread very thin and spread very lightly with Mayonnaise dressing. Rub to a paste the yolks of four hard boiled eggs with two tablespoons of melted butter. Season with salt and white pepper. Spread between the slices of bread. These are very nice for a lunch.

Cheese Sandwiches.

Chop three ounces of cream cheese very fine, then mix it to a paste with a teaspoonful of essence of anchovy and one tablespoon of butter. Spread on thin slices of bread, place them together and serve them garnished with parsley and water cress.

Hash.

Take equal parts of chopped potato and chopped meat, or two parts of potatoes to one of meat; season with pepper and salt. Put in enough hot water to cover the bottom of the spider; add one large tablespoon of butter. When the butter is melted, add the hash and let it simmer until a brown crust is formed; fold like an omelet. A little chopped onion can be added if desired.

Corn Beef Hash.

Take materials left from a boiled dinner. Take one part chopped corned beef to two of chopped potato, carrot, cabbage and turnip. Take one-third more potato than the other vegetables; season with pepper, and if not moist enough, moisten with the liquor in which the meat was cooked.

LADIES Look Here.

Why do you work and worry over your preparations for

Receptions.

Parties, Etc.,

when you can be served much better, without trouble and but a trifle more expense, by going to

DORSETT

and have him provide you all

Refreshments, Lunch and Card Tables, Chairs, Linen, China, Silver,

AND EVERYTHING NEEDFUL.

Read This Clipping:

"A long felt want has been supplied in the opening of the lunch parlors at Dorsetta's, the caterer on Nicollet avenue, as it provides a place where ladies can be pleasantly served. The new menu consists of hot and cold meats, potatoes, soups and all the essentials for a tempting meal. The rooms are already popular as ice cream parlors and the new feature is meeting with widespread approval among business men also."—*Tribune.*

It will Interest You.

Now the next time you are shopping call and take lunch at Dorsett's.

TRY SOME OF HIS CHOICE

Rolls, Cakes, Bon Bons, Delicious Ice Cream,

Fruit Sherbets and Confectionery.

YOUR PATRONAGE IS INVITED.

418 Nicollet.   **Dorsett, The Caterer.**   712 Hennepin.

Meat Pie.

Take cold meat, beef, turkey, veal or lamb, left from dinner; remove all gristle and fat, and cut in thin slices; put in a pudding dish and cover with the gravy left or with tomato; spread mashed potatoes that are left from dinner over the meat. Cover with beaten egg and cracker crumbs, and bake twenty minutes.

Meat Pie.

Take nice slices of any kind of meat left from dinner. Cook it up in the gravy or water, thickened a little. Add a little chopped onion and potato, a sprig of parsley chopped well, a little sage and pepper, and salt to taste. Cover with a nice baking powder crust. Make large incisions in the top and bake in a hot oven thirty minutes. Look in pastry for a recipe for the crust for a meat pie.

Scalloped Mutton.

Take cold roast mutton and cut in thin slices; season with salt and pepper; butter a dish; put in a layer of bread or cracker crumbs, a layer of meat, a layer of oysters, then tomato, and lastly a layer of meat and crumbs. Season each layer with pieces of butter and pepper and salt; moisten with gravy left over or stock of some kind. Macaroni can be used in place of oysters.

Turkish Rice.

One cup of stewed and strained tomatoes; to this add a cup of stock seasoned with salt, pepper and a little minced onion. While boiling add a cup of rice; stir lightly and add the last thing a large piece of butter; steam twenty minutes in a double cooker; serve as an entree or a garnish for fried chicken.

Dutch Cheese.

Place the milk in a pan on the back of the stove and scald it until the curd separates from the whey; strain in a cloth and wring quite dry. Put in a bowl, and with a large piece of butter, salt and a cup of cream; mix to a smooth paste. Roll into small balls, and put in a cool place; season with sage if you like the flavor. There should be at least ten quarts of lobbered milk. 2m

---

☞ Use Chap-O-Lene for all roughness of the skin.

☞ THE lady of the house is requested to read the recipe on page 32.

☞ Ladies will find Chap-O-Lene an indispensable article for the toilet.

Dumplings.

One pint of flour, half a teaspoon of soda and a teaspoon cream of tartar or heaping teaspoon of baking powder, one teaspoon of sugar, half a teaspoon of salt, one teacup of milk, one egg. Drop by spoonfuls into the soup or turn out on the board and cut into small cakes. Do not let the soup cease boiling while the dumplings are in it; they require about fifteen minutes. Do not let the steam escape but keep covered closely. Another recipe for dumplings is, two eggs, a cup of sweet milk and enough flour to make a stiff batter.

Balls for Soup.

Egg balls are made by mxing enough corn starch with two raw eggs to make into round balls. Drop in the soup and cook ten minutes.

Force meat balls.—To a pound of chopped beef or veal add one egg, a lump of butter, a cup of bread or cracker crumbs; season with salt and pepper and moisten with some of the stock in which the meat was cooked. Make into balls and fry brown in hot lard.

Lobsters.

When lobsters are purchased alive tie the claws together and plunge into boiling water—about a gallon—in which is a tablespoon of salt and a teacup of vinegar. Boil for thirty minutes. It will be a bright red. Drain, break off the claws and tail, remove and throw away the soft fins which lie under the legs. Shake out the coral and tomalley. Draw the body from the shell, split the lobster through the center and with a fork pick the meat from the joints. Cut under side of the tail shell, open and take out meat whole. Remember that the stomach is found near the head and is a small sack in which is poisonous matter and should be removed, also the dark vein found in the tail. The lobster can be seasoned and prepared in different ways.

Oyster Dressing.

Take one pint of finely grated or sifted bread crumbs, add three tablespoons of chopped suet or butter, a spoonful of mixed herbs, half a teaspoon each of salt, pepper and nutmeg; add one pint of oysters cut in two pieces or finer, and lastly two well beaten eggs. If not moist enough add sweet milk. Mix smoothly and stuff turkey or chicken with it.

☞ THE Swinburne Printing Company would like to see you when you have any use for printer's ink.

PASTRY.

USE best butter or lard. Cottosuet is excellent for pie crust and very digestable. Always have your shortening fresh and solid. With the exception of mince pies, pastry should be eaten the day it is made. Make enough paste to use at once; if any is left over keep it in the ice chest. Always mix the under crust a little stiffer than the upper with flour, this prevents the juice from soaking into the crust. Some use a beaten egg and rub it over the crust before putting in the filling. Always wet the edges of the lower crust with water or beaten egg, this causes the upper crust to adhere to the lower and prevents the juice from running out. Have the oven hot when the pie is first put in; this bakes the lower crust and prevents the crust from being soggy and raw. Remove from the tins as the crust is apt to become damp and taste of the tin. Always make opening in the upper crust, this lets out the steam, and especially so in meat pies of any kind. In making meringues for pies add one tablespoon of sugar to the white of one egg. Full the upper crust on a little as it shrinks in baking. Pies should be baked from half to three-quarters of an hour; mince pies, and pumpkin or squash require a good hour and a slow fire.

Good Pie Crust.

Take two heaping spoonfuls of lard or butter to one cup of flour, and a pinch of salt. Cut well into the flour with a knife, and wet with water to make a stiff dough. Mix as little as possible. This is enough for the upper and under crust of one pie. Use cottosuet in place of lard.

Pie Crust. 2.

To one pint of sifted flour add one even teaspoon of baking powder, a little salt, and sweet cream enough to make a stiff paste. This is enough for two pies.

Pie Crust. 3.

One-half cup flour before sifting, one-half cup of butter or cottosuet, three tablespoons of water and a pinch of salt. In mixing the shortening and flour use a knife. Dredge with flour and roll your under crust stiffer with flour than the upper.

Puff Paste.

One quart of flour, three-quarters of a pound of butter or lard, yolks of two eggs, teaspoon of salt, tablespoon of powdered sugar. Mix with ice water in a cool place. Place flour on the board, sprinkle over the salt and sugar, and egg gradually, beaten up with a little ice water. Mix until it becomes a smooth dough.

Apple Pie.

Line a pan with crust; pare and slice three or four good sized apples and spread evenly on the crust. Sprinkle with a small cup of sugar, bits of butter and sift a little cinnamon over it all; dredge a little flour over the pie and about three tablespoons of water. If the apples are not very sour squeeze the juice from part of a lemon in the pie. Add upper crust and press edges firmly together. Bake in a hot oven.

Dried Apple Pie.

Put your apples—enough for a pie—in warm water, and soak over night. In the morning stew a few minutes; add a little sliced lemon, and sugar to taste. Put in the pie and sprinkle a little flour over the apple, and bits of butter.

Crab Apple Pie.

Slice the crabs very thin, and make the same as the first recipe for apple pie. Add a little more sugar, as they are apt to be more tart than apples. These make a very rich pie, unequaled in flavor to any other kind of apple pie.

Apple Shortcake.

Line a tin with any kind of crust. With a soft cloth cover with melted butter; put on the top crust and bake. Slice and cook your apples, sweeten and flavor with a little cinnamon or nutmeg. Separate the upper crust from the under crust, and fill with the apple. Replace the crust, and serve with sweetened cream. In place of apple fill with fresh berries or sliced peaches.

Cream Pie.

To one pint of milk add a pinch of salt, and a teaspoon of butter. Let the milk come to a boil; add the yolks of three eggs well beaten with a small teacup of sugar and two even tablespoons of cornstarch. Bake your under crust; fill with the custard and spread over the whites well beaten and sweetened with two tablespoons of sugar. Brown in a quick oven.

Cream Pie. 2.

Pour a pint of cream upon upon a large cup of sugar; let it stand awhile. Beat the whites of three eggs; add this to the cream, and beat well. This will make two pies without upper crusts.

Custard Pie.

For one pie use three eggs to a pint of rich milk, a pinch of salt and a small teaspoon of butter, one-half cup of sugar. Let it bake until it custards, but does not water.

Cocoanut Pie.

One pint of milk, one cup of cocoanut, three eggs, one cup sugar. Use the whites for a meringue for the top. Bake with an under crust only. Instead of the dessicated cocoanut one cocoanut can be grated and used.

Lemon Pie.

One lemon; grate the rind, and squeeze out all the juice; put all in a bowl and pour over it one cup of boiling water. When cool strain, and add the yolks of two eggs, a small piece of butter, one cup of sugar, two teaspoons of corn starch. Bake your under crust, fill with the custard; spread on the whites beaten to a stiff froth and sweetened with two tablespoons of sugar. Return to oven and brown.

Lemon Pie. 2.

One lemon grated rind and juice, yolks of three eggs, teaspoon of of butter, three tablespoons of milk, one teaspoon of cornstarch, one cup of sugar. Prepare as the recipe above says, leaving out the boiling water.

Pie Plant Pie.

Cut up pie plant in small pieces enough for one pie; add one well beaten egg, a large cup of sugar. Mix well. Put in the crust and bake slowly about three-quarters of an hour.

Squash Pie.

A good cup of stewed and sifted squash, two eggs, one-half cup of sugar, butter size of an egg, one pint of sweet milk, one-half teaspoon each of cinnamon, cloves and nutmeg. Beat all together, and add milk; warm and bake in a deep tin with a rich under crust.

Rice Pie.

One-half cup of boiled rice, one cup of milk, one-half of sugar, two eggs, large piece of butter. Flavor with a little cinnamon, and put in a handful of raisins seeded. Bake with under crust only.

Pumpkin Pie.

Cut a pumpkin into thin slices, and boil until tender in as little water as possible. Stir often to prevent its scorching. Mash the pumpkin and let it stand on the back of the stove until all the water has dried away. Rub through a sieve. Add sugar enough to sweeten it well, a lump of butter, a teaspoon each of cinnamon, ginger and cloves, one nutmeg. Let it cook slowly. This will be enough for several pies and can be kept in the ice chest. For one pie take a large cup of the pumpkin, a pint of milk and one egg. (A little cream is nice.) Sweeten to taste. Bake with an under crust a good hour in a slow oven.

Pork Pie.

Line a pan with crust, pare and slice good, sour apples, put a layer in the bottom, seasoning with sugar and allspice. Shave very thin slices of salt pork, and put a layer on top of the apples, and pepper. Repeat this until the pan is full. Cover with a crust, and bake two and one-half hours.

Mince Meat.

Boil six or eight pounds of good beef tender. Take off scum as it rises, and salt just before it is done. Put away to cool. Remove all bones and bits of gristle, chop very fine. Make the mince meat in the proportion of two bowls of chopped apples to one of meat, and one cup of suet chopped fine. To this add the grated rind and juice of a lemon, a cup of molasses, cup of brown sugar, one quart of cider, one-half pint of boiled cider, one pound of raisins chopped and seeded, one-half pound of currants, one large teaspoon each of cinnamon, cloves and nutmeg, one-fourth pound of citron, teaspoon of salt, a little black pepper. A pint of cranberries cooked and put through a sieve gives a nice flavor. Cook this preparation until all the apples are cooked. It requires a good hour or longer. If not juicy enough add syrup from sweet pickles, or canned currants. This quantity, doubled and put away in a jar in a cold place, will keep all winter. For baking take out enough for a pie; if not moist enough add the juice of some kind of canned fruit. If none is to be had, a little hot water. If not sweet enough sprinkle on a little more sugar, bits of butter, a few whole raisins, and lastly two tablespoons of brandy. The brandy adds greatly to the flavor of the pies. In making this mince meat one must be guided by their own judgment as to sweetness and seasoning. Mince pies must be baked in a slow oven some length of time, at least an hour. Do not make too rich a crust for them, as they are rich in themselves.

THE WEINHOLD DRUG CO.

Platt's Chlorides,
The Household Disinfectant.

An odorless liquid. Powerful, Reliable, Prompt, Cheaper than Chloride of Lime or Carbolic Acid. Indorsed by 23,000 physicians. Daily employed by hundreds of thousauds of careful housekeepers.

Sold in Quart Bottles only, by Druggists Everywhere.

PREPARED ONLY BY

HENRY B. PLATT, 36 Platt St., Now York.

COTOSUET

Washington Pie.

Cup of sugar, one egg, small half cup butter, one-half cup sweet milk, two teaspoons baking powder, two cups of flour. Bake in two layers, and fill with jelly or jam. Sprinkle powdered sugar on top, and serve when partly cold as a dessert.

Cranberry Pie.

Bake two crusts, using any recipe for nice rich crust. Put bits of butter between so as to separate easily. Cook cranberries, enough for a pie; sweeten to taste just before removing from the fire. Place the jelly between the crusts when slightly cooled. Sprinkle powdered sugar on top.

Peach Cobbler.

Take one quart of flour, add one-half cup of butter or lard, salt, two teaspoons of baking powder. Mix with either milk or water. Mix soft, and line a dish with an under crust. Put melted butter between, and lay on an upper crust. Bake, and when done, split open and fill with peaches, sliced and sweetened, or any kind of fresh fruit. Serve with cream. Whipped cream is delicious placed on the top.

Chopped Cranberry Pie.

One quart of cranberries chopped, add two cups of sugar and half a cup of molasses. Dissolve one tablespoon of corn starch in a little cold water, and add one and one-half cups of boiling water. Stir all together, and bake with two crusts. This will make three pies. Divide the recipe for one large pie.

Sweet Potato Pie.

When the potatoes are dry and mealy, take a quart after they have been pared, boiled and mashed; add a quart of milk, four eggs, a little salt, cinnamon and sugar to taste. Bake with one crust. Half of this will make one good pie.

Short Cake.

One quart of flour, two heaping teaspoons of baking powder, half a cup of butter, two tablespoons of sugar, a little salt, enough sweet milk to make a soft dough. Roll soft; do not mix. Roll in two layers and place pieces of butter between so they will separate easily. Bake in a quick oven. Spread fruit between the layers and on top. Sprinkle with sugar, and serve with whipped cream. This will make four layers if desired. Strawberries, raspberries or peaches can be used for fruit.

Berry Pie.

Always allow two heaping spoonfuls of sugar, one teaspoon of corn starch or one tablespoon of flour to one pie. Put your berries in the tin lined with an under crust, and sprinkle sugar and flour over them. Use your judgment as to quantity of sugar according to their tartness or juiciness. Gooseberries and cranberries or green grapes require a large quantity of sugar. Press the two crusts together firmly to prevent the juice from running out. Some take a strip of clean white cloth wet and fold around the edge. When the pie is taken out strip off the cloth, and the edge is nice and brown, not burnt. In using canned fruit use very little sugar, and a little more flour.

Gooseberry Pie.

Take gooseberries, either green or ripe, and stew a little until they break. Sweeten well; dredge with a very little flour, and bits of of butter. Pour in a pie tin lined with paste, and cover with an upper crust. Green currants can be used this way also.

Crust for Meat Pies.

One quart flour, one pint of sour milk, a large teaspoon of soda sifted in the flour, and two tablespoons of butter or lard. Mix soft. Or the above recipe can be used.

Tarts.

Make a nice puff paste, roll out thin; cut with biscuit cutter. Cut out the center of some of them and lay on the large ones. Fill with jelly or jam.

2t

Log Cabin Maple Syrup.

HAVE YOU ASTHMA OR BRONCHITIS?

Dr. R. Schiffmann, St. Paul, Minn., will mail a trial package of "Schiffmann's Asthma Cure" free to any sufferer. He advertises by giving it away. Never fails to give instatnt relief in worst cases and cures where others fail. Name this Cook Book and send address for a free trial package. Weinhold Drug Co. always keep a supply in stock.

No ashes are lighter than those of incense, and few things burn out sooner.
—Lander.

☛ EVERY business man can profit if he will carefully follow the recipe on page 32.

☛ HIGH class printing and engraving. The Swinburne Printing Company.

☛ Caswell's Pectoral Balsam is a perfect cough cure.

PICKLES.

PICKLES are considered indispensible on a table. Pickles are made from almost everything in the shape of vegetables and fruit. Any kind of fruit that can be preserved is nice for sweet pickles, including the rind of water melons, and ripe cucumbers. Home-made pickles are the best; for usually the best vinegar is employed in making them, and good cider vinegar is very necessary to the best pickles. Never use any thing but a porcelain kettle in making them. Keep in a dry cool place. If a white mold appears on the top of the vinegar scald the vinegar over, and put in pieces of horse-radish or mustard seed. Seal sweet pickles while hot. In cooking sweet pickles cook until they can be easily pierced with a silver fork. In making a syrup for sweet pickles use three pints of best brown sugar to a quart of cider vinegar. If ground spices are used tie them up in a little bag, and throw into the hot syrup. Watch them closely and as soon as a white scum appears scald again, and if necessary add more vinegar, sugar and spices. Whole cloves and stick cinnamon are the only spices necessary.

Pickled Beans.

Take young butter beans and cook until tender. Put in brine made of one cup of coarse salt and two quarts of water. Let them stand a day or so. Take out and drain. Take two quarts of good cider vinegar, add a spoonful each of pepper, ginger, cloves and mace. Boil the vinegar and pour on the beans while hot. Pour off and boil the vinegar for two days in succession and put back on the beans.

Pickled Beets.

Boil fine, red beets until they are tender. Put in cold water, and slip off the skin, and cut in slices or any shape. Cover with a vinegar made the same as for beans. A cup of sugar can be added.

To Appreciate Good Cooking

One must be in a good state of health. Is it necessary to go to a doctor for every little ache and pain? If you do he will laugh at you and charge you a good, round fee. How can this be avoided? By keeping in your house a line of good family remedies, that have stood the test of many years, being used by millions for all ordinary complaints. There are many lines of family medicines, but the one that stands head and shoulders above all others in this country is "Dr. Ward's," manufactured by The J. R. Watkins Medical Company, Winona, Minn. Read what the people have to say about

Dr. Ward's Vegetable Anodine Liniment

WADENA, MINN., Oct. 31, 1893.

I have used Dr. Ward's Liniment for four years, and have found it a great benefit to my family. It beats anything I have ever obtained for vomiting in children. It is also very good for colic and pains. In fact, it is the best general purpose medicine I have ever had in my house. It has saved me some doctor bills. I would not be without it as long as I can get it.

Yours respectfully,
A. P. JOHNSON.

HENIFER, UTAH, Dec. 2, 1893.

Having used your liniment for about two years, for a number of diseases, such as bad colds, cuts and bruises; also for pains in the bowels, coughs, colic, cramps and many other diseases common to humanity, I can highly recommend it to any person who wants to use a first-class remedy. Thanking you for the great good you are doing humanity, I remain,

O. H. R. STEVENS.

BRANDON, BUCHANAN Co., IOWA, Dec. 18, 1893.

I have taken six bottles of your Gen-De-Can-Dra for the blood, and I think it the best patent medicine I ever took for a blood purifier. I have HAD RHEUMATISM FOR OVER THIRTY YEARS, and never had anything to help me as it has.

Yours truly,
F. W. THATCHER.

Dr. Ward's Gen-De-Can-Dra, For the Blood.

Dr. Ward's Petro-Carbo Salve.

MANLIUS, BUREAU CO., ILL., Jan. 15, 1894.

I write you in regard to your Petro-Carbo Salve. I think it is THE BEST SALVE ON RECORD for cuts, old sores, bruises, galls and anything that a salve is wanted for. It just fills the bill. I would not be without it in the house for twice the price of it. In fact I keep a supply of all your remedies, and find them all that they are guaranteed to be. You can use this if you see fit.

Yours truly,
SAMUEL L. BROWN.

FOR SALE BY **THE WEINHOLD DRUG CO.**

Cucumber Pickles.

Take one peck of small cucumbers. Select all about the same size. Put in a stone jar and sprinkle on the top a large cup of salt, and enough boiling water to cover them. Let them stand a day or so. Drain off the water and put the cucumbers on the stove in cold vinegar. Let them come to a boil. Add to the vinegar a cup of brown sugar, a few slices of green and red peppers, a piece of horse-radish, a few sticks of cinnamon, a few whole cloves, and some whole mustard seed. These pickles can be either kept in a stone jar or sealed up while hot in bottles.

Chow Chow.

Take half a peck of small cucumbers and let them stand in brine for several days. Put on two quarts of vinegar in which has been thrown a tablespoon each of mustard seed, celery seed, three green peppers, a few small onions and a little piece of alum. Boil the pickles twenty minutes in it. Add to the vinegar two pounds of sugar. Scald the vinegar over for three mornings. Take four ounces of mustard, and mix with the vinegar; add the pickles and put them away in a cool place.

Small, green tomatoes, beans, small white onions, mixed with small cucumbers can be made into pickles the same way. An ounce of tumeric adds to pickles.

Tomato Pickles.

Take one peck of green tomatoes and six large onions. Slice them and put on them a cup of salt, and let them stand over night. Drain well, and cook them in a gallon of cider vinegar, two pounds of brown sugar, half a pound of mustard seed, two green peppers chopped fine, a tablespoon each of allspice, cinnamon, cloves and ginger. Boil twenty minutes.

Chopped Pickles.

Take a peck of green tomatoes and chop them fine. Mix two cups of salt with them, and let them stand over night. Drain thoroughly; cake three times as much chopped cabbage. Let the cabbage stand with salt on the same time as the tomatoes. Cover each with vinegar and let them stand awhile longer. Mix together by putting in a jar in layers, and on each layer put chopped green peppers, whole mustard seed, horse-radish, cayenne pepper. Cover with a gallon of hot cider vinegar in which has been put a cup of sugar. A few onions chopped fine can be added.

☞ How to make Us happy, read the recipe on page 32 and follow it.

Ripe Cucumber Pickles.

Cut ripe, solid cucumbers into long pieces, about three inches long. Remove all seeds. Cook in water and salt until tender. Soak in alum water over night, using a lump of alum the size of a hickory nut. This hardens them, and makes them firm. Drain well and pour over them a syrup made of three pints of sugar to a quart of vinegar. Add stick cinnamon, whole cloves and mace; about two tablespoons of each. Scald the syrup and replace it on the pickles three mornings in succession. Then seal and put in a cool place. Be careful not to cook too soft. Use about a tablespoonful of salt to two quarts of water.

Water Melon Pickles.

Pare off the green rind, and cut in oblong pieces. Make and prepare the syrup the same as the above recipe says. Take off all of the red part of the melon. Pickle only the white rind. If a scum rises skim the syrup.

Peach Pickles.

Pare freestone peaches. Put in a jar and pour over them a syrup made of three pints of sugar to a quart of vinegar. Skim the syrup well, and pour on the fruit boiling hot. Repeat this for several days. Put pieces of cinnamon and cloves between the layers of peaches and stick some of the whole cloves in the fruit. Lastly scald the fruit, vinegar and spices together. Have the fruit the same color throughout. If there is not syrup enough to cover them well prepare more.

Pear Pickles.

Cut the fruit in halves and pare if large, if small leave whole. Prepare and make the same as peach pickles.

Spiced Currants.

Put a tablespoon each of cloves, cinnamon, mace and allspice in a bag and boil with four pounds of currants, two of sugar and one pint of vinegar. Some add a pound of raisins. Seal while hot in glass jars. Spice blackberries the same way; do not use quite so much sugar. Leave out the spices if one prefers.

2w

☞ THE place to get high class printing is at 9-11-13 Washington avenue north.

☞ THE housekeeper should not fail to study page 32.

☞ Caswell's Beef, Wine and Iron is the Ideal Tonic.

☞ Chap-O-Lene will positively cure chapped or rough skin.

PRESERVES AND JELLIES.

THESE are usually prepared with equal weights of sugar and fruit. Most people prefer preserves not so sweet, and use three-quarters of a pound of sugar to a pound of fruit and even less. Prepare the syrup and clarify it, then put in the fruit. Fruit like quinces, citron, melon rinds, cherries, currants, etc., harden if first put into the syrup. Cook in a little water until tender, or in a weak syrup first, then add them to the syrup. In very soft ripe fruits pour the boiling syrup on them and let them stand over night. The secret of keeping fruit is to have the covers of the cans fit securely, and keep the fruit in a dark, cool place.

In jellies extract the juice first by cooking the fruit in just enough water to keep it from burning, and strain the juice through a coarse flannel or cotton bag. Hang the bag over the kettle and let it drain. The rule is usually equal measures of fruit and sugar; sweeten less if preferred. Boil juice first, skim and add the sugar and boil until it jellies when a little of it is cooled. When jelly is put away cover the top with pieces of writing paper brushed with the white of an egg. Some use a little butter to grease the papers or wet them in brandy.

Citron Preserves.

Pare off the rind and cut in thin slices two inches long. Add equal weights of sugar and fruit and boil twenty minutes. Before adding the sugar boil the citron in a little water, tender; add two sliced lemons to each pound of fruit. Remove the fruit and boil the syrup down some, put in the fruit and boil awhile and seal in cans or jars.

Peach Preserves.

Pare the peaches and remove most of the pits; leave some to give the syrup a flavor. Make a syrup of three-quarters of a pound of sugar to one of fruit. Add water enough to dissolve the sugar. Skim and clarify. Add the fruit in small quantities at a time and cook eight to ten minutes. Skim out in a jar and put in more fruit. When all done fill the cans with the syrup and seal securely. A good plan is to pour off the syrup the next day and scald, and return to the can.

Pear Preserves.

Pare, cut in halves, prepare and make exactly the same as peach preserves.

Plum Preserves.

Take plums, wash them and prick each plum and put them in a stone jar. Make a thick syrup of equal weights of sugar and fruit. Pour the syrup on the fruit, and let it stand over night; repeat this for three days. Put fruit and syrup in a porcelain kettle and boil for an hour. Put in stone jars.

Quince Preserves.

Pare, core and quarter or slice your quinces; boil till tender in a little water. Take out and drain. Add equal weight of sugar to the water, replace the fruit and boil until clear. Take equal parts of quinces and quarters of nice sweet apples and preserve as for quinces. Cook the parings and cores and use the water for jelly, or add it to the sugar for the syrup of the quinces.

Tomato Preserves.

Take green tomatoes that are just beginning to turn; if red a little all the better. Pare and slice. Take equal weights of sugar and fruit and cook all together until the syrup is thick. Add one or two lemons sliced for additional flavor.

Cider Apple Sauce.

Pare and quarter nice sweet apples, put them in boiled cider enough to cover them and boil until tender. Any kind of apples can be used.

Apple Jelly.

Wash and quarter large crabs; cook in water enough to keep them from burning. Cook to a pulp, strain according to directions. Take three-quarters of a bowl of sugar to a bowl of juice. Boil the juice twenty minutes; add the sugar and boil five minutes longer. Try it to see if it jellies.

Preserved Berries.

To preserve strawberries, raspberries, currants, cherries or blackberries, take a bowl of fruit and a bowl of sugar. Dissolve the sugar in a very little water and add the fruit; cook until soft; skim as it needs it. Cherries should be stoned, but use some of the pits for flavor.

☞ THE cook will find something interesting on page 32.

Brandy Peaches.

Prepare peaches as the recipe for preserved peaches says, and just as the syrup is removed from the fire, add half a cup of brandy to a pound of fruit.

Grape Jelly.

Rub the fruit through a sieve; add a cup of sugar to a cup of pulp or three-quarters as much sugar as pulp. Boil the juice twenty minutes, and add the sugar. Boil until it jellies.

Quince Jelly.

Use the best parts of the fruit for preserves, and cook the skins, cores and hard part of the quince for jelly. Boil in enough water to cover. Mash and drain. Add equal weight of sugar and juice. Boil until it jellies.

Currant Jelly.

Do not have the currants over-ripe. Take equal parts of red and white currants if you can get them. Pick over and remove all leaves and poor fruit. Mash them in a kettle and drain in a flannel bag for several hours. Take a bowl of sugar to a bowl of juice. Boil the juice twenty minutes. Skim thoroughly; add the sugar and boil five minutes longer; turn into glasses and let them remain where the sun can shine on them several hours before sealing. Cover them with a paper dipped in brandy.

Berry Jam.

Pick over and mash the fruit; allow a pound of sugar to a pound of fruit. Boil until the jam looks dry and glistening, and no moisture gathers. This answers for raspberries, strawberries or blackberries. Equal parts of red and black raspberries make delicious jam.

Grape Jam.

Stew the grapes in a little water and press the fruit through a colander, adding a little water to get all the pulp through. Add sugar and make like the jam above. This answers for plums and gooseberries.

Wine Jelly.

Dissolve one box of gelatine in one pint of cold water; add four coffee cups of sugar and the juice and rind of two lemons; a little stick cinnamon. Let the gelatine stand an hour; add the sugar, lemon, three pints of boiling water and one pint of sherry. Strain into molds and let it stand until thick.

DR. SCOTT'S ELECTRIC HAIR CURLER — GIVEN AWAY.

At the urgent solicitations of many of our patrons and agents, we have just produced this new and beautiful Electric **"High Hip"** Corset. To quickly introduce it to readers of the Common Sense Cook Book, The Pall-Mall Electric Association of London and New York, make the following offer: If you cannot get it at your nearest store, remit at once the price, **$1.25**, with **15 cents** added for postage and packing. We will then send you (FREE) with the Corset, one of Dr Scott's **Electric Hair Curlers**, retailing at 50 cents, and **"The Doctor's Story,"** an invaluable book (price, 25 cents). It is an improvment over any other "High Hip" Corset ever made, both in elegance of shape and quality of material and finish. In shape it is French, in quality and finish it excels the English styles. United with all this they possess the marvelous virtues of Electro-Magnetism peculiar to all of Dr. Scott's Electric Corsets. Therefore with this combination of excellencies they are unrivalled. Avail yourself of this offer **NOW**.

It is made of fine Alexander cloth in drab and white, in sizes 18 to 30 inches, it is an unusually strong and durable article, and a perfect fit. It possesses strong Electro-Magnetic curative qualities and as such is cheap at $5.00. We invite you to make a test of these wonderful Corsets.

The price of this Corset is **$1.25**, but to those Ladies remitting for it we will forward as below.

So that for the amount you remit you receive $2.00 in value.

This offer is made to introduce this Corset to the readers of the Common Sense Cook Book.

"The Doctor's Story" is an eminently interesting work.

$1.25.

The cut below illustrates Dr. Scott's **Electric Curler**. It is remarkably popular with Ladies and Gentlemen. By its aid the hair or beard can be curled in any desired style in from one to two minutes. It produces the "Langtry Style," the "Patti Bang," the "Montague Curl," and any other form desired by ladies wearing their hair in the fashionable "loose and fluffy" mode Those who wear crimps or other forms of false hair will find this Electric Curler a very useful article. It does **not break off** and ruin the hair like the ordinary crimping process, and in wet and hot weather it works as quickly as in cold.

1 Corset, Retail,		$1.25
1 Hair Curler, Retail,		.50
1 "Doctor's Story," Retail,		.25

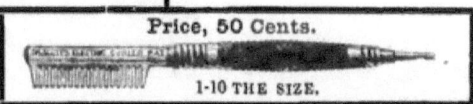

Price, 50 Cents.

1-10 THE SIZE.

DR. SCOTT, New York: LONDON, ENGLAND.
Your "Crimper and Curler" works charmingly. Its effect causes universal admiration. They are most simple to use. I consider them worth a guinea apiece to those who devote much attention to the ever changing arrangement of the hair.
L. LANGTRY.

Remit price to Dr. Scott, 842 Broadway, New York, and to insure safe delivery, add 15 cents for postage. Remit in Post-Office Money-Order, Draft or Currency in Registered Letter, payable to

GEO. A. SCOTT, 842 Broadway, N. Y.

Cranberry Jelly.

Prepare the juice as given in the directions; add four cups of sugar to every quart of juice. Cook until it jellies; make it sweeter if you prefer it very sweet. The above is very nice for cold meats.

Orange Marmalade.

Choose fine oranges, about a dozen; put them whole in a stew pan with water enough to cover and stew until tender. Change the water two or three times. Drain; take off the rind, remove the seeds and boil ten minutes longer. Add the peel cut in strips and boil a few minutes longer. Add the juice and grated rind of two lemons; cool and put away. 3a

---

Log Cabin Maple Syrup.

☞ ADVERTISERS are requested to read the recipe on page 32.

What's in a Name?

"No," said the fair young maid, as she listened to congratulations tinctured with malice, envy and all uncharitableness; "Guggenheimer is neither a beautiful nor a distinguished name. But when it goes with one of the largest ready-made pants businesses on West Broadway, it's a very reasonably decent sort of a Christmas present; and I want you to understand that I've got it."

☞ Caswell's Blood Cleaner will purify the blood.

FEW love to hear the sins they love to act.—Shakespeare.

☞ The Swinburne Printing Company, 9-11-13 Washington Ave. N., high class book and job printers.

A Master of Fiction.

Applicant—I understand you have a place for a writer of pure fiction.
Publisher—I have. Are you one?
"I think so."
"What have you done in that line?"
"Written several books for railroads, descriptive of the attractions of their summer resort regions, and—"
"That is sufficient! You may go to work at once."

☞ Chap-O-Lene, for the complexion.

As Far as the Surprise Went.

"And you really were surprised, Henry, dear?" said the young wife, gazing fondly into his eyes.
"Yes, indeed, dear," he replied with emphasis, as he gazed upon the pattern of the smoking-jacket; "I might even say startled."—Judge.

☞ High class work pays. When in need of anything in the printing line, call on The Swinburne Printing Co., printing, lithographing, embossing, book-binding, paper-ruling. 'Phone 253.

> This world is but a paradox.
> And plainly does this show
> In the fact that the surest "coming man"
> Is the man with lots of go.
> —Albany Times.

PUDDINGS.

PREPARE your butter, eggs and sugar as for cake. Do not put in too much sugar, as it is apt to make the pudding heavy. Puddings are either boiled, baked or steamed. If boiled use a bag made of fine drilling with a tape run in the top, or a tin mold with a cloth tied securely over it. Always flour your bag or cloth tied over the mold. Let the water entirely cover the bag; leave space in the bag or mold for the pudding to swell; turn it over frequently. Boiled puddings require more time than the others. Rice, bread and fruit puddings require a slow fire, and some time in baking. Batter and corn starch puddings, a quick oven. Steaming answers all purposes and is the most convenient and wholesome. Have your water boiling and steamer hot when the pudding is first put on, and do not let the water stop boiling. Replenish if necessary from the tea kettle in which the water is hot. Do not uncover and allow the steam to escape until the time is up. If these directions are followed a light, wholesome pudding is the result, if not, a soggy, heavy one.? In making custards for puddings bring your milk to a boil, and then add your sugar and salt, and lastly, the well beaten eggs. If corn starch is used, either dissolve in a littld cold milk or stir thoroughly in the sugar; otherwise the mixture will be lumpy. Stir constantly and cook always in a double cooker; add your flavorings after removing from the stove. Beat yolks and whites separately. To keep your custard from curdling a good plan is to add your sugar to the boiling milk and then the eggs.

Apple Pudding.

One egg, small half cup of butter, one cup of sugar, cup of sweet milk, level teaspoon of soda, and two of cream of tartar, or in place of sweet milk use sour milk, or butter milk, and one-half a teaspoonful of soda. Line sides and bottom of a pudding dish with quarters of apples; pour on the butter, and bake in a quick oven half an hour. Serve with a cream or common sauce. (See sauces.)

Apple Dumplings.

Make a crust of one pint of rich butter milk, one teaspoon of soda, and a quart of flour, pinch of salt. Roll half an inch thick. Cut dough in four inch squares. Lay several slices of apples on them, sprinkle over a little sugar, cinnamon, and pieces of butter. Roll up and tuck in the ends. Prick deeply with a fork. Bake in a brisk oven until the apples are well cooked. Serve with a whipped cream sauce, or sweetened cream. A baking powder crust can be used.

Apple Koker.

One teaspoon of salt, two teaspoonfuls of baking powder, two cups of sifted flour; sift all together. Rub in a lump of butter, one egg beaten light, and a cup of milk. Roll half an inch thick, and place in a shallow baking pan. Press down quarters of apples placed in parallel rows on top of the dough, edge down. Sprinkle sugar over the apples, and a little cinnamon. Bake twenty minutes, and serve with a common sauce.

Apple Betty.

One cup of bread crumbs, two cups of chopped tart apples, one-half cup of sugar, two tablespoons of butter, one-half cup of water. Butter a deep dish, put apples and brumbs in alternate layers. Sprinkle the sugar, and bits of butter, and a little cinnamon over the apples. Finish with a layer of crumbs. Cover closely and bake in a moderate oven three-quarters of an hour. Uncover and brown quickly. Eat with cream or sweet sauce flavored with lemon.

Delicious Bread Pudding.

Two cups of finely sifted bread crumbs, one quart of milk, yolks of four eggs, piece of butter size of an egg. Beat yolks, add milk and crumbs and butter; grated rind of one lemon. Bake half an hour. Do not let it remain in the oven too long or it will be watery. Spread with a layer of jelly and cover with a meringue made of the whites of the eggs flavored with the juice of half the lemon. Return to oven, and brown. This can be served alone or with a hard sauce. (See sauces.)

Cottage Pudding.

One cup of milk, two eggs, one cup of sugar, two cups of flour, three tablespoonfuls of melted butter, two teaspoonfuls of baking powder. Bake in a bread pan and cut in small squares, and serve with common sauce flavored with lemon juice, or a fruit sauce.

☞ ARE you going to lay this book down and not read that recipe on page 32.

Corn Starch Pudding.

One pint sweet milk, two eggs, two tablespoons corn starch, three tablespoons of sugar, pinch of salt, teaspoon of butter. Let milk come to a boil, dissolve the corn starch in a little of the cold milk, beat eggs and sugar together; add to the hot milk, and cook in a double boiler five minutes; eat with sweetened cream flavored with vanilla. A cocoanut or chocolate pudding can be made of this recipe by adding one cup of grated cocoanut, or for a chocolate pudding add one-fourth a cake of chocolate dissolved in the milk.

Cocoanut Pudding.

Grate half a cocoanut; make a custard of a quart of milk, four eggs, a teacup of sugar and piece of butter size of an egg. Bake with an under crust half an hour. Eat with the following sauce:

Sauce.—One-half cup butter, one cup of sugar, and one cup of wine. Put all in a bowl of hot water. Do not stir. The above is good without sauce.

Cracker Pudding.

One cup of finely rolled cracker crumbs, one pint of milk, yolks of two eggs, pinch of salt, a lump of butter. Bake twenty minutes. Do not let it remain in the oven too long. Spread a layer of jelly on top and add the whites of the eggs, beaten to a stiff froth with two tablespoons of sugar. Return to oven and bake brown. Flavor meringue with vanilla.

Bird's Nest Pudding.

Six or seven apples pared and cored. Put in a pudding dish and pour over them a custard made of one pint of milk, three eggs and five teaspoonfuls of flour and a little salt. Bake an hour and serve with hard or cream sauce.

Cranberry Pudding.

One cup of milk, spoonful of butter, two tablespoons of sugar, two teaspoons of baking powder, a little salt, one pint of flour, one egg. Grease teacups, put a few cranberries in the bottom, then a spoonful of the butter, and so on until the cup is nearly full; steam in a steamer three-quarters of an hour. Serve with a common or cream sauce. Put in other layers of fruit such as canned peaches, blueberries, raisins, etc.

☛ Try Caswell's Blood Cleaner.

☛ Good printing is to a business what good clothes are to a man. The Swinburne Printing Co. can give you entire satisfaction. 'Phone 253. Ring 'em up.

Crow's Nest Pudding.

Melt a piece of butter the size of an egg in a pudding dish. Peel and slice six large tart apples, cover with one cup of sugar. Make a batter of one cup sour cream, one-half teaspoon of soda and a pinch of salt; flour enough to make a thin batter. Pour on the apples and bake nearly an hour. Serve with sweet cream.

Blueberry Pudding.

Sprinkle a buttered dish with bread crumbs and a layer in the the bottom; put in bits of butter, then a layer of blueberries, another layer of crumbs and butter and so on until the dish is full. Bake half an hour. Serve with sweet cream or sauce made as follows:

SAUCE.—Half a cup of cream, a half cup of milk, teaspoon of corn starch, two tablespoons of sugar and a half teaspoon of vanilla. When nearly cold stir in an egg well beaten. Pour on the pudding and serve. Any kind of fruit, raspberries, fresh or canned, dried apple sauce flavored with lemon, or strawberries, can be used in place of blueberries.

Graham Pudding.

Half a cup of molasses, two tablespoons of butter, one egg, half a cup of milk, half teaspoon of soda, two cups of Graham flour, one cup raisins, and spices to taste., A little sliced citron or figs can be used. Flour the fruit and add last. Steam three hours. Serve with foaming sauce.

Delicate Pudding.

Boil one cup of water with one cup of fruit juice, (orange, lemon, canned raspberries, quinces, currants), add three tablespoons of corn starch wet with a little cold water. Cook ten minutes. Salt and sugar to taste. Beat whites of three eggs and stir in. Turn in a mold and serve cold with a boiled custard sauce. (See boiled custard.)

Pineapple Pudding.

Take one pineapple cut in thin slices and sprinkle one-half cup of sugar over it. Let stand for an hour. Make a custard of one quart of milk, three tablespoons of corn starch, four eggs, (the yolks), cup of sugar. When cold pour over the pineapple and add a meringue made of the whites of the eggs. Brown in the oven. Oranges can be sliced and used in the same way; only do not let them stand with sugar on, and use half the amount of sugar.

☞ Your attention is respectfully called to page 32.

NO MORE GRAY HAIR.

BRUCELINE, the only genuine remedy for restoring gray hair to its natural color; no dye and harmless.

BRUCE'S HAIR TONIC cures baldness, strengthens the hair, prevents it from failing out, removes dandruff and diseases of the scalp.

Treatise on the hair sent free on application.

PRICE PER BOTTLE, $1.00. Druggists or THE BRUCELINE CO., 377 6th Av., near 23d St., N. Y. Thousands of Testimonials.

FOR SALE BY

THE WEINHOLD DRUG CO.

Fruit Pudding.

One cup of molasses, one of sweet milk, one cup of suet, chopped very fine and shredded well, one cup of stoned and chopped raisins, one-half cup of chopped figs, one-half cup of currants, two and a half cups of flour, half a teaspoon of soda, salt and add one teaspoon each of cinnamon, cloves and nutmeg. Flour the fruit well and add last. Stir well and steam two hours. Serve with brandy sauce. This is a very nice pudding and will keep for weeks in a cool place.

Simple Fruit Pudding.

Butter slices of bread, spread with apple jelly. Put in a pudding dish with layers of dried or canned fruit, apricots, peaches or raspberries. Pour over it a boiled custard and bake, adding the whites for the top.

CUSTARD.—One pint of milk, yolks of three eggs, three tablespoons of sugar, pinch of salt, one-half teaspoon of vanilla. Follow directions for making custards.

Christmas Pudding.

Two cups of raisins, one cup currants, two cups of apples peeled and chopped, two cups of finely chopped suet, a pint of bread crumbs, four eggs, cup of sugar, half teaspoon of salt, one nutmeg, one teaspoon each of cinnamon and cloves, two large cups of flour. Flour the fruit from this. Either boil in a bag or steam in a pudding tin two hours. Serve with any sauce given. Brandy or wine are the nicest.

Rice Pudding.

Half a cup of rice, one quart of milk, half teaspoon of salt, one cup of sugar, half cup of whole raisins, a little cinnamon or nutmeg. Bake slowly two hours. Stir once or twice at first. Eat with hard sauce flavored with lemon juice.

Apple Tapioca Pudding.

Half a cup of tapioca. Soak over night in a quart of cold water. Put in a double boiler and cook until clear. Add one cup of sugar, piece of butter, teaspoonful of lemon juice. Pare four good sized sour apples, take out core and pour the tapioca over them, and bake an hour. Serve with cream and sugar, or whipped cream sauce.

Baked Fruit Pudding.

One cup milk, one cup flour, two eggs, tablespoon of butter, little salt, one cup of fruit, either apples or peaches. Put batter in a pudding dish and sprinkle in the fruit. Serve with foaming sauce.

Indian Pudding.

One quart of milk, two heaping tablespoons of Indian meal, four of sugar, one of butter, three eggs, teaspoon of salt. Heat milk, pour in meal slowly, cook a few minutes; add butter and pour on the egg, sprinkle in a little cinnamon and cloves or nutmeg. Bake in a slow oven an hour.

Steamed Indian Pudding.

Scald a half pint of meal with half cup of boiling water, add two tablespoons of Graham flour, one cup of milk, either sweet or sour, one tablespoon of molasses, half a teaspoon ginger, one teaspoon of cinnamon; a little salt, level teaspoon of soda, two tablespoons of chopped suet or butter. Steam two hours in a well greased pudding dish. A half cup of currants can be added if desired. Serve with any kind of sauce.

Dried Apple Pudding.

One cup dried apples, cup of molasses, one and a fourth cups of flour, one-fourth cup of butter, one egg, one teaspoon each of soda, cinnamon and cloves. Soak apples over night; cut fine and mix with the water in which they were soaked, add egg, sugar, butter and flour. Stir soda with the molasses and apples. Steam or bake. Serve with common sauce, or cream sauce.

Yorkshire Pudding.

For every teacup of sweet milk, take one egg, one and one-half cups of flour, pinch of salt, and a heaping teaspoon of baking powder. Stir to a smooth batter, and pour in a roasting pan under roast beef half an hour before it is done.

PUDDING SAUCES.

In making sauces, if corn starch or flour is used, mix thoroughly with the sugar while dry. This will keep lumps from forming. Do not boil the sauce after the butter is added. If brandy or wine is used, flavor after removing from the fire. If the juice or rind of a lemon or orange is used put in just before removing, as boiling with any of the grated rind is apt to make the sauce bitter. Do not make your sauce until ready to serve.

Whipped Cream Sauce.

Two cups of whipped cream, one cup of powdered sugar, white of an egg beaten to a stiff froth. Flavor with vanilla, lemon or wine.

Foaming Sauce.

One-half cup of butter, one cup of sugar, white of an egg beaten to a foam, three tablespoons of wine or two of brandy, one-fourth of a cup of boiling water, one teaspoonful of vanilla.

Common Sauce.

Melt one heaping tablespoon of butter, two teaspoonsful of flour and a cup and a half of hot water; add a cup and a half of sugar, and two tablespoons of lemon juice.

Hard Sauce.

Cream equal parts of sugar and butter and flavor with lemon juice or add a little nutmeg and cinnamon. Rub butter to a cream and add sugar gradually.

Brandy Sauce.

One cup and a half of sugar, one heaping tablespoon of butter, one level tablespoon of corn starch, cup and a half of boiling water. Boil sugar and corn starch dissolved in a little water, add butter, and remove from fire. Put in three tablespoons of good brandy.

Cream Sauce.

One-fourth cup of butter, one-half cup granulated sugar, two tablespoons of wine, two tablespoons of cream. Cream butter, add sugar, then wine, and lastly cream. Cook in a double cooker. Use lemon or vanilla in place of wine.

Wine Sauce.

One cup boiling water, one tablespoon of corn starch, one-fourth cup of butter, one cup of powdered sugar, one egg, one-half cup wine. Wet the corn starch in a little cold water, and stir in the boiling water. Boil ten minutes. Rub butter to a cream; add sugar, then egg and wine, and pour all into the water and corn starch. Stir well.

Molasses Sauce.

One cup of molasses, half a cup of water, one tablespoon of butter, three tablespoons of vinegar or lemon juice, a little cinnamon or nutmeg. Boil all together for twenty minutes and serve at once.

Chap-O-Lene for the hands.

POND'S EXTRACT
WILL CURE

FAC-SIMILE OF BOTTLE WITH BUFF WRAPPER.

Sore Throat,
Lameness,
Influenza,
Wounds,
Piles,
Earache,
Chilblains,
Sore Eyes,
Inflammations,

Hoarseness,
Frost Bites,
Soreness,
Catarrh,
Burns,
Bruises,
Sore Feet,
Face Ache,
Hemorrhages.

AVOID IMITATIONS.   ACCEPT NO SUBSTITUTE.

POND'S EXTRACT CO., 76 Fifth Avenue, New York.

Caramel Sauce.

Put one cup of sugar in a small frying pan, and stir until it is a light brown. Add a cup of boiling water, and cook slowly fifteen minutes. Add a little lemon juice, and some of the rind or a piece of stick cinnamon. Strain and serve hot.

Fruit Sauce.

One cup of sugar, large tablespoon of butter, one small tablespoon of flour, cup of hot water. Mix the flour with the butter and stir until a light brown, add sugar and water, and lastly half cup of canned currents or any kind of jelly. Canned raspberries are very nice in place of currants.

After the first trial every lady will appreciate

COTTOSUET.

For Drugs, Medicines, or anything found in a well appointed

Drug Store, go to

THE WEINHOLD DRUG CO.

SAUCES AND CATSUPS.

Lobster Sauce.

ONE small lobster, four tablespoons of butter, two of flour, a little cayenne pepper, two tablespoons of lemon juice, one pint of hot water. Rub flour and butter together; add water, pounded coral and seasoning. Cook five minutes, and serve strained on the lobster. This will do for all kinds of boiled fish.

Tomato Sauce.

One can of tomatoes. Cook in it a small slice of onion, two tablespoons of butter, two of flour, a few cloves. Heat butter and flour together, and stir in the tomatoes. Season with salt and pepper. Strain and serve with any kind of meat or fish.

Tartare Sauce.

The yolks of two eggs, three tablespoons of vinegar, a little mustard, teaspoonful of sugar, a little pepper and salt to taste. Add a tablespoon of onion juice. Add the last thing two tablespoons of butter or half a cup of oil. Chop a tablespoon of capers, and add a tablespoon of cucumber pickles after they are chopped. Serve with fried fish and meats in jelly.

White Sauce.

One pint of milk, one cup of cream, four tablespoons of flour, yolks of two eggs, salt and pepper. Put the cream and milk on in a cooker. Put in the flour rubbed smooth in a little of the milk. Stir awhile, and cook ten minutes. Add the yolks of the eggs, and remove from the fire. A tablespoon of parsley can be added. This is nice for salmon, cod or halibut.

Mushroom Sauce.

Take one pint of stock, two tablespoons of flour, three of butter, salt and pepper to taste. Melt the butter, add the flour, and stir until brown; add the stock and a can of French mushrooms. Cook five minutes. This is nice served with beef.

Cream Sauce for Vegetables.

One cup of milk, teaspoon of corn starch or flour, two tablespoons of butter, salt and pepper. If you have cream use it in place of butter.

Sauce for Fried Fish.

Two tablespoons of butter heated in a frying pan. Add a tablespoon of chopped parsley, tablespoon of lemon juice, teaspoonful of vinegar, salt and pepper. Pour over the fish before sending to the table.

Chili Sauce.

Take twelve large, even-sized, ripe tomatoes, three green peppers, two onions, two tablespoons of salt, three of sugar, one of cinnamon, pint and a half of vinegar. Peel tomatoes and onions and chop fine. Chop the peppers and boil all an hour and a half. This can be doubled. A quart can of tomatoes can be used in place of ripe ones.

Tomato Catsup.

Take four quarts of tomatoes. Stew and run through a sieve. Do not allow any of the seeds to go through. Boil the pulp down to jelly. Be careful not to scorch it. Add a gallon of vinegar, four tablespoons of salt, four of black pepper, two of allspice, three of ground mustard, a little cayenne, one tablespoon of cinnamon and a teacup of sugar. Bottle while it is hot and seal securely. If one likes onion add half a dozen small ones to the pulp and cook with it.

Holland Sauce.

Put in a sauce pan two large tablespoons of butter, the juice of a lemon, the beaten yolks of two eggs, a speck of cayenne, half a cup of boiling water, salt and pepper to taste. Stir until it thickens. Strain and serve with baked fish.

Mint Sauce.

One cup of fresh chopped mint, two tablespoons of sugar, one-half a cup of vinegar. Let it stand an hour, and serve with roast lamb.

Horse Radish Sauce.

Cream two tablespoons of butter, add two tablespoons of grated horse radish, a tablespoon of thick cream, and half a teaspoon of vinegar. Stir in a little salt and a teaspoon of ground mustard. Keep on the ice till thick and cold. Serve with any kind of cold meat. 3k

---

$500.00 Reward for any adulteration found in Log Cabin Maple Syrup. Ad. on page 62.

Bread Sauce.

One pint of milk, two tablespoons of fine bread crumbs, two tablespoons of chopped onion, one tablespoon of butter, salt and pepper to taste, one cup of coarse crumbs. Boil the fine crumbs, and fry the coarse crumbs in the butter. Pour the sauce on the game and sprinkle over the brown bread crumbs.

TO CURE HICCOUGH.—It is not generally known that a piece of loaf sugar will instantly stop the most troublesome hiccough.

CANDIED LEMON PEEL.—This is made by boiling lemon-peel with sugar, then exposing it to the air until the sugar crystallizes.

Bed bugs, according to a lady correspondent, have a great aversion to salt. She states that if the articles and places infested with bed bugs are washed with salt water, and the crevices in which the vermin hide are filled with it, they will give no more trouble.

LOCK JAW.—The following is well worth saving for future reference: "Locked jaw from a rusty nail in the foot was entirely cured in four cases reported by Dr. Kinkle, by applying to the whole spinal column cloths saturated with chloroform, just at the approach of the spasm. It was repeated at several returns of the spasm, always inducing sleep and finally recovery."

A young man out west was intrusted with the money to bring his father home a good family sewing machine. He carried off a neighbor's daughter to Chicago, married her, brought her home and said: "There, father, is the best one I could find."

A pretty girl and a wild horse are liable to do much mischief; for the one runs away with a fellow's body, and the other runs away with his heart.

EXTREMES.—Many a fool has passed for a clever man because he has known how to hold his tongue; and many a clever man has passed for a fool because he has not known how to make use of it.

☞ Try Caswell's Blood Cleaner.

☞ Gentlemen will find Chap-O-Lene very beneficial applied immediately after shaving.

☞ The only concern in the city making a specialty of high class printing, engraving and embossing is The Swinburne Printing Company.

☞ Caswell's Pectoral Balsam cures all coughs, colds and affections of the throat, chest and lungs.

SALADS.

SALADS should come to the table fresh, crisp and cold. To crisp lettuce, celery or cabbage place them in the ice chest some time before serving. Never press down a salad to get it into form. In arranging the salad toss it lightly with a fork. Do not cover a delicate salad with hard boiled eggs or boiled beets, etc. Reserve these for chicken, veal or turkey salads. Use the white leaves of the celery, and the light green leaves of the lettuce. Always tear lettuce, do not cut it. Wash it thoroughly, as hot house lettuce is very apt to be covered with little green lice. Always wash all vegetables thoroughly. Cut chicken with a knife not to fine. Shave cabbage with a sharp knife, and cut your celery into small pieces. This is better than chopping it. Rich salads like chicken, veal, salmon, lobster, and shrimp are not served after meats at dinner, but are only appropriate for lunch or tea. Vegetable salads, like lettuce, cucumber, potato, tomato or cabbage are the best after meats. Do not add the dressing until the salad is ready to be served. Salads can be garnished with pieces of jelly, celery heads and the heart of the lettuce. Use slices of lemon for all kind of fish salads. Asparagus, string beans and peas must all be boiled in salted water until tender before using. In mixing dressings, if hard boiled eggs are used powder them with the back of a spoon; beat raw eggs very light, add oil, and lastly vinegar. A dressing should be ice cold before putting on the salad. When oil is used pour in a drop at a time beating well all the time. A nice way to serve fish salads is in shells in each of which is placed a leaf of lettuce. Chicken salad can be served in a salad dish or enough for one individual can be placed in a shell made of two leaves of lettuce and served from a platter. Use the Mayonnaise or cooked dressing with all kinds of meat or fish salads. For green salads use a plain or French dressing.

Salad Dressing. 1.

Mash the yolks of two hard boiled eggs, add one teaspoon each of mustard and salt, a little cayenne pepper and a pinch of black pepper, piece of butter size of an egg, or three tablespoons of olive oil, yolk of one raw egg, one-half cup of vinegar. A tablespoon of sugar improves it. This is excellent for any kind of a salad.

French Salad Dressing.

One salt spoon of salt, one-half salt spoon of pepper, three tablespoons of oil, one tablespoon of vinegar. If you like the flavor of onion, add one tablespoon of onion juice. This can be obtained by grating the onion with a coarse grater. To prepare this put the salt and pepper in a cup, add the oil slowly, and then the vinegar. This is nice for lettuce or potato salad.

Simple Salad Dressing.

Three eggs, one tablespoon each of sugar, oil and salt, small tablespoon of mustard, cup of milk and one of vinegar. Stir oil, sugar, salt and mustard until smooth, add eggs and vinegar and lastly milk. Put in a bowl and place in boiling water until it thickens. This is enough to use several times.

Cream Salad Dressing.

One-half cup of vinegar, a piece of butter the size of an egg, yolk of one egg, a teaspoon of mustard, half a teaspoon of salt, a little cayenne pepper, two tablespoons of sugar. Cream sugar, butter, mustard, egg and salt together; add vinegar and put in a bowl in boiling water until it thickens like custard. Remove and add two tablespoons of thick sweet cream. This is excellent for cabbage or lettuce salads or any kind of a salad.

Quick Salad Dressing.

This can be made at the table. Yolk of an egg, tablespoon of mustard, pinch of salt, six tablespoons of olive oil, tablespoon of lemon juice. Stir yolk, mustard and salt until they thicken, and add oil drop by drop, stirring all the time.

Mayonnaise Dressing with Butter.

The yolks of two eggs, one level teaspoon of salt, one of pepper, two of white sugar, two teaspoons of mustard, one tablespoon of butter, four tablespoons of vinegar. Stir mixture thoroughly. Put in a bowl in hot water and stir until it thickens, and then set away to cool.

Mayonnaise Dressing. 2.

Beat the yolks of three eggs very light, add a tablespoon of sugar, tablespoon of mustard, a little cayenne pepper, teaspoon of salt. Beat all to a cream, put in a bowl set in ice water and add a pint of olive oil, dropping in gradually a few drops at a time until the mixture is thick and very hard. Thin with half a cup of vinegar and juice of half a lemon. A cup of whipped cream makes it very nice, but can be omitted without injury to the dressing. This can be doubled for a large company.

Chicken Salad. 1.

Free one cold boiled or roasted chicken of bones and skin. Cut the meat into little dice or long strips. Season with salt and pepper. There should be a quart. Have a pint of nice tender celery, cut into small pieces about half an inch thick. Mix with the meat and when ready to serve pour over it a Mayonnaise dressing. Garnish with slices of hard boiled eggs or dices of beets. Serve on a platter, putting enough for one individual on one of the large leaves of the lettuce.

Chicken Salad. 2.

Cut up one chicken, using only the tender meat, add one cup of cabbage, shaved very fine with a sharp knife, and one cup of celery cut in small pieces. Pour over it a Mayonnaise dressing (see Mayonnaise dressing with butter). Serve in a salad dish garnished with the green leaves of the celery and the small leaves of the lettuce.

Turkey Salad.

This is especially nice in preparing for a large company. The meat takes the place of chicken and is just as nice. Make the same as chicken salad, using half cabbage and half celery. Garnish with slices of cold hard boiled eggs and the green leaves of the celery.

Lettuce Salad.

Wash each leaf carefully. Drain and keep in a cool place until ready to serve. Put the leaves in a salad bowl, the light ones in the center. Tear some of the larger ones and arrange around these. Pour over all a French dressing. A cream dressing can be used if desired.

Always Fry Doughnuts in

COTTOSUET.

Ad. on page 22.

Cucumber Salad.

Take two cucumbers and cut off about one inch of the point. Cut in very thin slices, and soak in salt and water for an hour. Take two heads of lettuce, tear in small pieces. Drain the cucumber and put with the lettuce in a salad bowl. Serve with a French or cream dressing. Cucumber can be used without the lettuce.

Potato Salad.

Take one quart of potatoes cut in slices while hot. Cut in thin slices one or two onions, or use two tablespoons of grated onion; add a little chopped parsley. Pour over all any kind of dressing, enough to make it very moist. Place sprigs of parsley around the dish, and serve cold. Bits of cold fried salt pork or bacon are nice mixed with the salad.

Cucumber and Tomato Salad.

Place a layer of crisp lettuce in the bottom of a salad dish, a layer of sliced cucumbers prepared as the above recipe says, then a layer of sliced tomatoes. Pour either a French or Mayonnaise over the whole.

Tomato Salad.

Slice large tomatoes, arrange on a bed of crisp lettuce, sprinkle with a little sugar and pepper, and pour over all a cream dressing. Garnish with celery tips.

Salmon Salad.

Take one can of salmon, break in small pieces, add a little salt, pepper, half a cup of vinegar, throw in a few whole cloves, a little chopped onion if wished. Let this stand for two hours. Pour this off and put the salmon in a circle of lettuce leaves, and pour a Mayonnaise dressing over it. Garnish with hard boiled eggs, and slices of lemon. Fresh salmon can be used the same way. Celery can be used with the lettuce. Serve in shells lined with lettuce.

Lobster Salad.

Cut up the lobster like chicken, season with a French dressing. Let it stand until ready to serve. Then tear up one-third as much lettuce, mix with the lobster, and serve in a nest made of two large lettuce leaves. Mix half of the Mayonnaise dressing with the lobster. Put a tablespoon of the prepared lobster in the nest with a tablespoon of the Mayonnaise dressing. Serve in a platter. Garnish with parsley. A nice way to serve a small company is to serve the salad in shells for this purpose, in each of which is placed a leaf of lettuce. 3p

Oyster Salad.

Take a quart of oysters, and let them come to a boil in their own liquor. Season with salt, pepper, tablespoon of lemon juice,[and three tablespoons of vinegar. Put in the ice chest, and let them become thoroughly cold. Put in a bowl and stick in the little tender celery tops and some of the celery cut up. Pour over all a Mayonnaise dressing, and garnish with white celery leaves. Any kind of a dressing is nice with the oysters.

Cabbage Salad.

Take one quart of finely shaved cabbage and add two large slices of onion chopped fine. Take two tablespoons of bacon or fat pork, one teaspoonful of sugar, half a cup of vinegar, salt and pepper. Fry the onion in the fat; add the other ingredients until boiling. Pour hot over the cabbage and serve.

Cabbage Salad. 2.

Take equal parts of finely shaved cabbage and celery; pour on it a plain salad dressing. Garnish with the boiled whites of the eggs and the green leaves of the celery.

Shrimp Salad.

Take one can of shrimps, halve or chop them. Take one-half as much celery or lettuce; pour over all any kind of Mayonnaise dressing. Garnish with a border of lettuce leaves, or prepare the salad the same as for salmon salad. Serve in shells.

Bean Salad.

Cook string beans until tender in salted water; cut them in halves or quarters. Pour over them a French dressing and serve cold.

Beet Salad.

Take cold beets cut in small pieces. Mix with pieces of lettuce and garnish with celery tips. Pour over all dressing No. 1, or a French dressing.

Sardine or Fish Salad.

One quart of any kind of cold cooked fish freed from all bones. Place on a bed of crisp lettuce. Split six sardines and remove any bones. Place them in the center of the dish, cover with a boiled dressing or a Mayonnaise. Place slices of lemon around the dish and garnish with parsley or lettuce.

☛ Chap-O-Lene will positively cure chapped or rough skin.

Veal Salad.

Cook veal nice and tender, cut into dice and prepare the same as for chicken salad. This is an excellent substitute for chicken salad.

Egg Salad.

Boil six eggs twenty minutes. Cut the whites in small pieces; rub the yolks through a strainer over the whites. Pour over all a French dressing. Serve with balls of cottage cheese. 3r

---

WHAT MAKES A BUSHEL.—Wheat, sixty pounds; corn, shelled, fifty-six pounds; rye, fifty-six pounds; oats, thirty-two pounds; barley, forty-six pounds; buckwheat, fifty-six pounds; Irish potatoes, sixty pounds; sweet potatoes, sixty pounds; onions, fifty-seven pounds; beans, sixty pounds; bran, twenty pounds; clover seed, sixty pounds; timothy seed, forty-five pounds; hemp seed, forty-five pounds; blue grass seed, fourteen pounds; dried peaches, thirty-three pounds.

RHEUMATIC LINIMENT.—Benzine, four ounces; tincture camphor, two ounces; tincture opium, one ounce; chloroform, one ounce; mix. Apply by wetting a cloth or flannel with the liniment and laying on the affected part; then place a napkin, folded several thicknesses, over that, and bind or press it gently on as long as the patient can stand the burning sensation. It will not blister.

"Have the jury agreed?" asked the judge of a court attache whom he met on the stairs with a bucket in his hand. "Yis," replied Patrick, "they have agreed to send me out for a half gallon of whisky."

COMPARISON OF THE SEXES.—Women are said to have stronger attachments than men. It is not so. A man is often attached to an old hat; but did you ever know of a woman having an attachment for an old bonnet? Echo answers "never."

APOLOGIES FOR MARRYING.—Many strange apologies have been urged for marriage. Goethe said he married to gain respectability. Wilkes wedded to please his friends. Wycherly, in his old age, took his servant girl to spite his relations. The Russians have a story of a widow who was so inconsolable for the loss of her husband, that she took another to keep her from fretting herself to death.

☞ You are invited to call or write for samples of work when in need of anything in the line of high class printing, from a calling card to a three-sheet poster.—The Swinburne Printing Company, 9-11-13 Washington Avenue North.

GREAT NORTHERN SOAP CO.,
MINNEAPOLIS, MINN.

Have the sole right to manufacture W. A. Woodburn's

SPANISH SOTOLE SOAP.

This soap is made from pure material, combined with Sotole, or natural soap, from the Sotole plant and will excell all other soaps in cleansing qualities, and yet it possesses a mildness that will not injure any fabric. It also possesses great curative properties which make it very desirable for family use.

SPANISH SOTOLE LAUNDRY SOAP

Will wash all kinds of cotton, linen, silk, woolen and worsted goods, carpets and woodwork, better than any other soap.

SPANISH SOTOLE BATH AND TOILET SOAPS

Will be desirable for all toilet purposes, especially for those needing a healing soap for chapped hands, etc., such as mechanics, machinists, printers, farmers, and all others who desire a soap to remove stains and leave the skin soft and smooth.

SPANISH SOTOLE CURATIVE SOAP

Is a finer grade of soap, containing olive oil, and will cure eczema, rash, prickly heat, burns, etc., and is used for medicinal purposes.

SPANISH SOTOLE SILVER SOAP

Will clean all kinds of gold, silver, brass, tin, nickel, and will clean gilt picture frames and make them look like new.

Every housekeeper should keep a supply of these soaps.

All dealers in soaps will handle these goods. Try them, prove them, and you will continue to use them.

SOUPS.

SOUPS are made from meat, fish and vegetables, with water or milk. They are classified according to material, color, quality, etc. When soup is made of stock, meat is the basis. To make nutritious, healthful soups, requires study and practice. Always have materials on hand such as dried herbs, rice, okra, vermicelli, onions, carrots, whole as well as ground spices. Parsley is another necessary article. With these soups can be make from scraps of meat left from a meal. Pieces of steak, bones of roast beef or veal make a good stock. Save the water in which chickens, beef tongues or leg of mutton are cooked. The carcass of a turkey, in which are remnants of the dressing, cooked slowly makes an excellent soup. It is not necessary to buy meat expressly for the purpose of making soup stock.

By stock we mean a liquid containing the juice and soluble parts of meat and bone, which has been extracted by slow cooking. Stock made from meat without bone or gristle will not jelly when cold. Stock can be made from the cheapest inferior parts of meat, which yield the most nutriment when cooked. When buying meat for stock select a piece from the shin or lower part of the round of beef or veal. This has a bone with marrow, and a large proportion of gelatine. Stock made from roasted or browned meats is the most nutritious. A bay leaf adds greatly to the flavor of soup. Always put your meat or soup bone into cold water without salt, and let it cook slowly for several hours. Cover closely; thus keep the flavor of the meat from escaping with the steam, and also prevents it from being reduced too quickly by evaporation. Skim the stock several times, and when the meat is reduced to rags, strain, and put away in an earthen jar. When cold remove the grease from the top. This is the basis of several kinds of soups, and will keep in a cool place for some time. Soups can be served thin, or thickened with flour, corn starch and different vegetables. Do not put away stock with vegetables in it, as they are apt to sour it. For coloring soups brown, use caramel, browned flour and onions browned in butter. Caramel can be made by boiling one cup of sugar and two teaspoons of water in a sauce pan until brown; then add half a cup of water and boil for a few minutes. Serve soups with bread browned in the oven, and cut in small dice, or squares of bread thrown into boiling fat, and browned. Serve with oyster soup crackers crisped in a hot oven. Clear stock by removing the fat, and using the white of an egg for every quart of stock. Do not add the egg when the stock is hot, but set it on the fire and stir all the time, until it comes to a boil. A scum will form which when taken off leaves the liquid clear and sparkling. Always strain thoroughly. Cook your vegetables that require long boiling, as rice, sago, macaroni, tapioca, etc., separately, then add the stock. Serve with clear soups slices of lemon, yolks of hard boiled eggs, force meat balls, or a spoonful of grated Parmesau cheese on each plate. The nicest of clear soups is the French, called Consomme.

For five pounds of clear meat and bone use about six quarts of water. Add a pinch of sugar to all soups. Thick soups require more seasoning than thin ones. Never use any kind of meat that is the least bit tainted, as the stock witl taste of it. Cayenne pepper, Worcestershire, Halford or Chili sauces and catsup are used by some, but must be used cautiously. Wine is also used by some for the extra flavor. If soup is salted too much modify by adding a little sugar and a tablespoon of vinegar.

Asparagus Sauce.

Two bundles of asparagus, one quart of stock, one pint of milk, one cup of cream, three tablespoons of butter, three of flour, one onion, salt and pepper to taste. Cut off the tops and cook awhile in salted water; cook the remainder until done. Cut the onion in small pieces, and fry in the butter, add flour and then add the stock and asparagus. Boil twenty minutes, strain and add the milk and cream.

Bouillon.

Melt one tablespoonful of butter in a sauce pan, add one-half an onion sliced very thin. Cook until the onion is browned, then add one and one-half pounds of finely chopped beef (that from the round being best), one and one-half pints of cold water. Cover the pan and let all simmer gently for two hours. Strain, and return to the kettle, and boil Beat the white of an egg with one-half cup of water, add this to the bouillon, and boil four minutes, strain, and if it is too light add caramel, but have it very clear.

☞ WE guarantee our work. If it is not entirely satisfactory send it back: don't use it up and then ask for a rebate, as you won't get it. We don't care to deal with cranks. The Swinburne Printing Company.

☞ Child's Cough Cure is prepared especially for children.

Mock Bisque Soup.

Stew one pint of tomatoes for twenty minutes with one slice of onion, one bay leaf, and one sprig of parsley. Put through a sieve, and return to the stove. Rub one large tablespoon of butter, and two of flour to a paste, stir into one quart of boiling milk until it thickens. Add one teaspoon of sugar and one-half a teaspoon of soda to the tomato. Strain into the milk and serve at once.

Beef and Vegetable Soup.

Put a good soup bone on in cold water, about three quarts to a three-pound soup bone. Simmer slowly until the meat falls from the bone. Skim frequently as the scum rises. Remove the fat, which hardens when the stock is cold. Peel, wash, and slice three potatoes, cut up one-fourth head of cabbage, peel and slice two onions, one head of celery, and tomatoes if desired. Boil until done in the stock. Strain and serve. Some use carrots and turnips. Season with parsley, thyme and sage. Force meat balls are nice served with beef soup. Drop them in the soup just before serving.

Beef Soup.

Take bones and trimmings from a large roast of beef, two cold mutton chops, pieces of sirloin steak; add three quarts of water. Let this boil slowly until the meat is in rags. Strain and cool; remove fat and when ready to use heat to a boiling point, and add one tablespoon of salt, four cloves, one tablespoon of mixed herbs. If a cold fried egg, baked apples or cold boiled onions are found in the pantry add them to the stock. Boil a few minutes and strain and serve.

Bean Soup.

Take one quart of any good beef stock. Soak a coffee cup of beans two hours, and boil for an hour and a half. Add to the stock, and boil awhile. Season with salt, pepper and sprinkle in a few bread crumbs, and serve hot. If desired add three potatoes, a small piece of turnip and a parsnip, all cut up fine. An onion gives the soup a nice flavor.

Bean Soup Without Meat.

Boil one pint of beans in a quart of water; pour off the water, and add a fresh quart of water. Cook until very tender. Skim out half of them; to the other half add one cup of sweet cream or half milk and cream, butter size of an egg, pepper and salt to taste.

☞ THE Swinburne Printing Company would like to see you when you have any use for printer's ink.

Consomme.

Two pounds of shin of beef, two pounds of knuckle of veal, one fowl. Cook all in four quarts of cold water. Simmer until the meat is in shreds. Cut up three onions, one-half a carrot, one-half a turnip, and fry them in ham fat or the drippings. Strain the stock, when cold remove the fat; add the vegetables and season with a little celery, parsley and rind and juice of a lemon. Strain and serve clear. Clarify with the white and shell of an egg, as given in the preface. It should be transparent and of a light brown color. The stock from beef alone can be used.

Celery Soup.

Take one quart of milk, one small half teacup of boiled or steamed rice. Put in a steamer over boiling water. Cook five or six sticks of celery in a little water until tender; add to the milk and put in a piece of butter size of an egg, pepper and salt to taste. Cook over the water one-half an hour, and just before serving add one well beaten egg to the hot soup and serve hot.

Chicken Soup.

Take the broth left after boiling chickens to fry, or for a salad. Strain and add small pieces of the chicken. Season with salt and pepper and a little minced onion. Thicken if desired with one tablespoon of corn starch, or add two well beaten eggs. Boil twenty minutes and serve with slices of lemon.

Chicken and Beef Consomme.

Cut one pound of lean beef from the round into small pieces, add one pound of chicken bones. Cover with cold water and let it stand on the back of the stove and simmer for four hours. Add two slices of onions, a bay leaf, a sprig of parsley, slice of carrot and a piece of celery. Cook for an hour slowly; strain and let it cool. When cold remove the fat and heat when ready to serve. If not clear and brown, color and clear as directed in bouillon.

Duchess Soup.

Take one quart of milk and heat to the boiling point. Take two large onions and slice fine and fry in two tablespoons of butter; fry awhile and then add two tablespoons of flour. Stir all into the milk and cook ten minutes. Strain and return to the fire. Add two tablespoons of grated cheese, and the last thing three well beaten eggs. Season with salt and pepper. Do not boil after adding the eggs. The cheese can be omitted.

Clam Soup.

Twenty-five small clams, one quart of milk, half a cup of butter, one tablespoon of chopped parsley, three potatoes, two tablespoons of flour and salt and pepper to taste. Chop the clams fine and drain. Chop the potatoes and cook them in the milk. Rub butter and flour together and add to milk and potatoes. Add parsley, pepper and salt, and cook for awhile. The last thing add the clams. The liquor from the clams is not used. Cook the potatoes in the milk at least fifteen minutes before adding the other ingredients.

Lobster Soup.

One small lobster boiled in three pints of stock or water. Pound and use the coral if there is any. Cook three tablespoons of butter and three of flour together; stir into the soup and season with salt, pepper and a speck of cayenne. Boil a few minutes and strain. Add pieces of the lobster to the soup and serve at once.

Green Corn Soup.

Six ears of sweet corn or one pint of pulp. Boil the cobs in cold water thirty minutes and strain. Put the corn water on and add the corn pulp and cook fifteen minutes. Thicken with a tablespoon of flour and one tablespoon of butter cooked together. Add salt and pepper, a teaspoon of sugar, and just before serving add one pint of milk or cream.

Julienne Soup.

One quart of stock, and one pint of mixed vegetables, salt and pepper to taste. Cut celery, turnip, carrot, and onion into small dice and cook until soft. Add to the stock, and serve hot. In summer use green peas, asparagus or string beans.

Mulligatawney Soup.

Take chicken or turkey left from dinner, and scraps of roast veal, lamb or mutton; add four quarts of water. Cut up fine four stalks of celery, two onions, two slices of carrot, cook for twenty minutes in four tablespoons of butter; to this add two tablespoons of flour and one tablespoon of curry. Stir this into the soup and cook four hours; then remove and strain. Add a small cupful of barley, that has been simmering on the back of the stove for several hours, and bits of the chicken or turkey. Cook awhile and serve. 3w

DEMAND Log Cabin Maple Syrup.

Lamb Soup.

Boil a nice leg of lamb or mutton in three quarts of water. Use the water for the soup. Chop two onions and a potato fine, and two large tomatoes; add these to the soup and boil one hour. Have a half a cup of barley simmering on the back of the stove; add this to the other and boil fifteen minutes. Season with salt and pepper. This can be thickened if preferred by adding a tablespoon of flour wet with cold water.

Mock Turtle Soup.

Wash, clean and soak for awhile one calf's head. Remove the brain and tongue. Take four pig's feet, and the head, and boil in a gallon of water three or four hours, or until the flesh slips from the bones. Skim thoroughly. Add a tablespoon of salt. Remove the meat and put it where it will cool so as to cut up into dice. Keep the rest for force meat balls. Put the bones on to cook again, add six cloves, six allspice, stick of cinnamon, tablespoon of mixed herbs, two onions, one carrot, one turnip, one stalk of celery. Let this cook until all is reduced to two quarts. Strain and cool. Remove the fat when cool. Make a brown thickening of two tablespoons of butter, and two tablespoons of corn starch and one pint of brown stock. Stir this into the other stock. Add a cup of the meat cut into dice and finish the seasoning by adding the last thing a glass of sherry or Maderia wine and the juice of a lemon. Serve with sliced lemons and make force meat balls and throw into the soup five minutes before taking from the fire. Make the balls as follows: Rub the yolks of three hard boiled eggs to a paste, using the brains to moisten the yolks with; season with a little pepper, salt and lump of butter. Mix this with two well beaten eggs and with the hands mold into little balls, and throw into the soup a few minutes before it is done.

Noodle Soup.

Make noodles by adding to one egg as much sifted flour as it will absorb; salt and roll out thin; dredge with flour, roll over and over into a large roll. Cut into strips, shake out and drop into any kind of clear, thin soup.

Oyster Soup.

Two quarts of water, tablespoon of salt, two tablespoons of butter, pepper. Heat to the boiling point and add a pint of oysters. Skim carefully and add just before serving half a cup of sweet cream and a few crackers rolled fine.

☞Caswell's Pectoral Balsam is guaranteed to give satisfaction or money refunded.

Okra Soup.

Take two quarts of nice stock either made from a good beef bone or from chicken or turkey, add one quart of water, and salt and pepper. Fry one-quarter of a pound of salt pork out, and add one onion, and one quart of green okra cut into small pieces. Cover and fry half an hour. Add to this before removing two tablespoons of flour. Add this to the other ingredients; simmer two hours, strain and add any pieces of the chicken. Serve with a dish of steamed rice.

Milk Stew.

Three pints of milk to pint of oysters. Bring the milk to the boiling point and add the oysters. Skim and season with a large lump of butter, pepper and salt to taste. Do not let the milk boil and be very careful that it does not scorch.

Onion Soup.

Bring one quart of milk to the boiling point, put three tablespoons of butter in a frying pan; in it throw six onions sliced fine. Let them cook for some time. Add to the onions a tablespoon of flour. Turn this mixture into the milk and cook fifteen minutes; strain and season with salt and pepper. Beat the yolks of two eggs and add one cup of cream or milk to them, stir into the soup and serve hot. If you use milk instead of cream put in an extra lump of butter. The thickening can be left out.

Ox Tail Soup.

Take a couple of ox tails, skin, joint and soak them in lukewarm water for awhile. Chop up two onions, season with a little cayenne and allspice, add this to the meat. Bring them to the boiling point and skim; when the scum has ceased to rise cover and let them cook two hours. Strain and add two tablespoons of mushroom catsup, and a glass of sherry wine. Return the meat to the soup, boil together and serve with toasted bread.

Pea Soup.

Take two quarts of good beef stock, and in it boil one quart of green peas or split peas. If they are dry peas soak over night and boil until tender in just a little water. Add peas to the stock and cook until the peas are done enough to pass through a sieve. Strain through a sieve and season with pepper and salt. Let the soup simmer for thirty minutes and just before serving stir in a tablespoon of butter in which has been stirred a teaspoon of flour. A cup of cream stirred in just before serving improves it greatly. If you have no cream use milk and double the butter.

Potato Soup.

A quart of milk put on to boil with an onion and a stalk of celery. Pare six potatoes and boil thirty minutes; turn off the water and mash fine. Add the milk, pepper and salt to taste and a tablespoon of butter. Rub through a strainer; serve at once. A cup of cream greatly improves the soup.

Turtle Soup.

Take a can of green turtle. Take the green fat by itself and cut into little pieces. Boil the rest of the turtle in three pints of water. Season with six pepper corns, a few cloves, a sprig of parsley, and a little sage and thyme. Put a tablespoon of butter in a pan, and fry in it one large onion, a slice of carrot, one of turnip, and a little celery. Skim out these and add to the soup. In the butter left add a tablespoon of flour. Stir into the soup and cook slowly an hour. Strain and serve with the green fat. Four tablespoons of wine can be added if desired.

Tomato Soup.

A quart can of tomatoes or a quart of fresh tomatoes, one pint of water. Cook the tomatoes and water twenty minutes. Take a large tablespoon of butter, and fry in it one minced onion, and when brown add one tablespoon of corn starch; add to the tomato, and cook fifteen minutes. Strain through a sieve, and season with salt, pepper, and a teaspoon of sugar.

Milk Tomato Soup.

One can of tomatoes cooked twenty minutes in one pint of water. Add a small teaspoon of soda. Bring a quart of milk to the boiling point, season with butter, pepper and salt to taste. Add a little rolled cracker; add this to the tomato, and boil a few minutes and serve hot.

Turkey Soup.

Take the carcass of a turkey left from dinner and what remains of the gravy, dressing, bones, etc. Put in three quarts of cold water, and cook slowly for three or four hours. Strain and cool. Skim off the fat; pick off bits of the meat and add to the soup. Thicken if desired, with a little flour wet with cold water.

Vermicelli Soup.

Take a quart of good rich beef stock, and add one-half a cup of vermicelli broken up, and cooked in a little salted water about fifteen minutes. Season with salt and pepper. Macaroni can be used in place of vermicelli.

Vegetable Soup.

One-half a cup of chopped onion, one cup of cabbage, one-half a cup each of turnip and carrot, one cup of potato, a stalk of celery. Put all but the potato and cabbage into two quarts of boiling water, and cook thirty minutes; then add cabbage and potato, one teaspoon of sugar, salt and pepper to taste; one tablespoon of parsley and sage chopped fine. Cook thirty minutes and rub through a sieve. Add two tablespoons of butter, and a cup of sweet cream. This soup can be thickened by adding a tablespoon of flour fried in the butter.

Clam or Fish Chowder.

Three pounds of cod, bass or salmon, six potatoes, a piece of salt pork, two onions, tablespoon of salt, a little pepper, tablespoon of butter, quart of milk and six large crackers. Remove the scales. Wipe the fish carefully, and cut into pieces two inches square. Put the bones and head on to boil. Slice the potatoes, and parboil them. Fry the onions and pork fat and butter together. Strain the fat, leaving the onions. Put in the potatoes, and the water in which the bones were boiled. When boiling put in the fish, and add the milk. Split the crackers, and pour the chowder on them. If wanted richer stir in two eggs well beaten. Clam chowder is made the same way, using half a peck of clams in their shells in place of fish and using the liquor.

Barley Soup.

A teacup of barley, quart of chicken stock, one onion, a little mace and cinnamon. Cook barley several hours. Rub through a sieve, and add a pint of cream or milk. If it is milk add two tablespoons of butter. Salt and pepper to taste. Rice soup can be made by using rice in place of barley.

4a

Mrs. Masterman uses and recommends

COTTOSUET.

If your grocer don't keep it he can get it for you. Made only by

SWIFT & CO.,

South Omaha, Neb.

VEGETABLES.

BY VEGETABLES we mean such plants as are used for food, and comprise all parts of the plant from the root to the leaves. The fresher the vegetables are the better. They should be washed and cleaned thoroughly in cold water, and cooked in boiling water. Always salt the water in the proportion of a teaspoonful of salt to a quart of water. The time of cooking varies with the age of the vegetable. All should be cooked until tender, and no longer. String beans, turnips, parsnips, carrots and cauliflower require from one to two hours. Potatoes boiled require thirty minutes; baked forty-five. Onions are best put in warm salt water for awhile before cooking; this removes the strong odor. In cooking greens add salt and a pinch of soda to preserve the color. Add a pinch of soda always to any kind of beans. This removes the strong, beany taste. Old potatoes should be soaked in cold water some time before cooking. In cooking potatoes remove and drain as soon as done. Uncover a little to let the steam out, and place on the back of the stove to dry out. This makes them mealy. The secret of mealy potatoes is to cook them rapidly and remove and drain as soon as done. Try with a fork, and if soft, drain. Some prick baked potatoes as soon as done or squeeze a little. This lets out the steam and keeps them from being watery. Raw potatoes that are to be fried should be sliced thin, and soaked in cold water. This draws out the starch and makes them crisp instead of mealy.

Asparagus.

Wash and clean thoroughly. Use only the tender part of the stalk. Cut off any that is white. Boil in salted water. Boil the stalk first, and then throw in the tips. When tender season with a little cream, lump of butter and pepper to taste. The asparagus can be cooked whole and served with melted butter.

Asparagus on Toast.

Prepare as above, only leave the stalks whole. When tender put in a lump of butter, pepper and a little thickening if one likes it, and pour it over slices of toasted bread. The water must be boiled down so as to leave just enough for the gravy. Use a teaspoon of corn starch for thickening.

String Beans.

String by cutting off the ends of the pods. Cut in inch pieces or break. Boil from one to two hours until perfectly tender. Beans require longer time than most vegetables. Throw in a pinch of soda just before draining. Add a cup of cream or part milk, a piece of butter, salt and pepper to taste. Shelled beans should be prepared with the same kind of dressing, only they do not require as great a length of time to cook tender.

Baked Beans.

Pick over and wash one quart of beans, soak in plenty of water over night. In the morning pour off the water; cover with hot water and let them come to a boil. Pour off this water and add more. Boil until they begin to split. Put the beans in an earthen jar or crock always saved for this purpose. Throw in a pinch of soda. Put in the bottom one pound of good fat and lean salt pork. Mix a little mustard with two tablespoons of molasses, and a little water. Have water to cover the beans. Bake all day. Watch them and if they need any more seasoning and water add it. Some add a little chopped onion for additional flavor or put two slices of an onion on top of beans.

Boiled Dinner.

Use a nice piece of corn beef, put on in warm water and when it comes to a boil pour off the water and add enough more to cover well. Skim off the scum as it rises. Before the vegetables are put in remove the meat and put in vegetables as follows: Turnips cut in slices, cook awhile and then add cabbage cut in quarters, pototoes whole and a few carrots or parsnips. Beets should be boiled in some of the liquor separately. After removing the vegetables put in the meat for a few minutes to heat through. Serve cabbage and beets in separate dishes. Place turnips and carrots or parsnips on the platter with the meat. Season with butter, pepper and vinegar to suit the individual taste. Prepare the beets as the recipe below says. 4c

---

☞ WEDDING Invitations, Announcements, At Home, etc. High class work produced by The Swinburne Printing Company, 9-11-13 Washington avenue north.

☞ Chap-O-Lene for the hands.

Beets.

Cook whole. Do not break off fibers or roots, or peel, as the juices escape. Cook from one to five hours. When tender drop in cold water and slip off the skins. Slice in a dish, add pieces of butter, pepper and salt; pour over a little vinegar and let them stand in a hot oven a few minutes. Serve hot. Place some of the beets in vinegar and a few pieces of horse radish on top and let stand for a day or so for pickles.

Beet Greens.

Wash the young beets and tips very thoroughly. Cook in salted water with a piece of salt pork. Take out and drain and dress with butter, pepper and vinegar.

Corn Oysters.

One cup of flour, half a cup of butter, three tablespoons of milk, teaspoon of salt, pepper, one pint of grated corn. Pour corn on the flour, add the rest and fry in the frying pan in which is hot fat to the depth of two inches. Put in batter by spoonfuls.

Boiled Corn.

Clean off all the silk carefully and cut the heads off the cob. Boil in salt water three-quarters of an hour, or cut the corn (after it is cleaned) with a sharp knife from the cob. Stew with a little water. When tender add milk, butter, pepper and salt to taste. Beaten eggs added makes a rich dish.

Cauliflower.

Take off the green leaves and stalk, put on to cook in boiling water. Boil for an hour or longer until tender; pour off water and add a cream sauce. It is a good plan to let it soak in salt water before cooking.

Succotash.

Take equal quantities of shelled beans and corn cut from the cob. Cook each separately until tender. Mix together and season with cream and milk, a large piece of butter, pepper and salt. A little sugar if one likes it. Succotash can be made from canned corn and dry beans the same way. The beans must be soaked over night and boiled until tender before adding them to the corn. Season as above.

Cabbage.

Slice with a sharp knife very fine, put in a stew pan and add a little water. Cover closely and cook until tender. Add milk, butter, pepper and salt to taste, or a cream sauce.

4d

Fried Cabbage.

Slice cabbage fine, place in a pan in which are some pieces of bacon or salt pork, previously fried a little. Add a little water, cover closely and cook down until brown. Some add a little vinegar just before removing from the stove. Cabbage is considered indigestable, and some boil it with a small piece of red pepper and change the water once or twice. It is more wholesome served as a salad.

Celery with Cream Sauce.

Wash and scrape celery, cut in pieces two inches long. Boil half an hour, drain off water and add a cream sauce. (See sauces.)

Egg Plant.

Cut the plant in slices, pare these and cover with boiling water in which has been put a teaspoonful of salt; let this stand an hour. Drain, and pepper the slices and dip in beaten egg and bread crumbs. Fry the pieces in boiling fat. Or the slices can be fried in just enough pork fat or bacon to brown them.

Macaroni and Cheese.

Boil about four ounces of macaroni, broken up in small pieces in a little salted water about fifteen minutes. Grate a quantity of cheese. Put in an earthen dish a layer of macaroni, a layer of grated cheese, bits of butter, pepper and salt, another layer of macaroni, then cheese until the dish is full. Pour over it all enough milk and cream to come to the top. Bake slowly three-quarters of an hour.

Macaroni with Tomato.

Boil in a little salted water a little macaroni (about a cupful) a few minutes, pour over it a quart of canned tomatoes. Season with pieces of butter, salt, pepper, a little minced onion and sprinkle sifted bread crumbs on top. Bake in hot oven three-quarters of an hour.

Italian Macaroni.

Take a piece of beef, about two pounds, half a pound of salt pork, two chopped onions. Let all cook for awhile; add a quart of tomatoes, pepper and salt, and cook all for three hours. Boil a sufficient quantity of macaroni fifteen minutes, put a layer in a dish, cover with some of the mixture above, a layer of grated cheese and so on until the dish is filled. Bake an hour.

4e

☛—ANYTHING from a calling card to a large show card embossed in colors, or from a circular to a history of the world, can be produced by the Swinburne Printing Company, 9-11-13 Washington avenue north.

Boiled Onions in Cream.

Wash and peel, cook in salted water until tender; do not pour off all the water. Add a cup of cream or milk, piece of butter, and pepper and salt to taste.

Fried Onions.

Cut in thin slices, boil in a little salted water. Add a generous supply of butter or beef drippings; season. Cover closely and fry until brown.

Scalloped Onions.

Slice large onions in thin slices. Put in a dish a layer of bread crumbs, pieces of butter, pepper and salt, then a layer of the onion. Do this until the dish is full. Moisten with milk enough to fill up the dish. Bake an hour.

Green Peas.

Boil green peas until tender; drain. Put in a sauce pan two tablespoons butter, one of flour, a little sugar. Stir until well mixed; add a cup of cream, the peas and let all come to a boil.

Prepare canned peas in the same way. Leave out the thickening and sugar if one prefers.

Potatoes, Boiled or Baked.

Peel and put to soak in cold water. Select ones as near of a size as possible; leave the small ones to be cooked for mashed potatoes. Boil thirty minutes in boiling water in which has been thrown a handful of salt. Try with a fork and remove as soon as done. Drain and set on the back of the stove with the cover partly off to let the steam escape. Clean potatoes for baking with a small brush. Cut out all the black spots, and bake from half to three-quarters of an hour. Baked potatoes should not stand a moment, but be served immediately.

Scalloped Potatoes.

Take potatoes and slice thin, put in a dish in layers. Between put bits of butter, pepper and salt. Pour over enough sweet milk to fill the dish. Bake three-quarters of an hour. Cold boiled potatoes can be used in place of raw.

Lyonnaise Potatoes.

One quart of cold boiled potatoes cut into small slices, one chopped onion, three tablespoons of butter. Season with chopped parsley, salt and pepper. Fry onions in the butter, then add potatoes. Stir arefully so as not to break. Serve on a hot dish.

Mashed Potatoes.

After boiled potatoes are drained, mash thoroughly; add milk, cream, a piece of butter, and stir until smooth. The longer they are beaten the better. Put in a vegetable dish. Smooth and press down with a spoon and knife. Put bits of butter on top, and a little pepper. Place in a hot oven for a few minutes.

Potato Balls.

Take mashed potatoes left from dinner, mix with the yolk of an egg and a little flour, pepper and salt, a little chopped parsley and butter. If not moist enough add a little cream. Mold into balls with the hand, and fry or bake brown.

Creamed Potatoes.

Cut cold boiled potatoes into cubes or slices. Cover with milk, season with pieces of butter, salt, pepper and chopped parsley.

Saratogo Potatoes.

Cut in thin slices and fry in boiling fat. Skim out and put in a covered dish. Sprinkle over a little pepper and salt.

Sweet Potatoes.

These can be baked or boiled. They are the best baked. When cold they can be fried or creamed the same as other potatoes. They are nice cooked till tender and browned with roast beef.

Rice.

Rice should be thoroughly washed in several waters. It is cooked in several ways. It is the best steamed.

STEAMED RICE.—To one cup of rice add two cups of boiling water, and half a teaspoonful of salt. Cook in a double boiler half an hour. Stir with a fork to let the steam escape, and cover. Cook until the water is absorbed and the rice is tender.

Savory Rice.

Fry a tablespoonful of chopped onion in one of butter until yellow. Add one cup of uncooked rice. Then add one pint of chicken stock and steam thirty minutes in a double boiler. This is an excellent side dish. Season if desired with cayenne pepper, chopped parsley and herbs.

☞ Caswell's Blood Cleaner will purify the blood.

☞ Use Chap-O-Lene for all roughness of the skin.

Squash.

Squash can be either steamed or baked. If steamed remove from shell, and mash and season with a liberal supply of butter, a little pepper and salt. If baked, cut in small pieces and serve. Let each individual season his own to taste.

Turnips.

Cook these from one to two hours. Cut in thin slices. Mash fine and season with butter, pepper and salt. Some pour white sauce over them.

Parsnips.

These, to be fit to eat, should remain in the ground during the winter. Boil, cut into half-inch pieces and serve with cream sauce, or fry pieces in frying pan with lard or drippings.

Tomatoes.

Scald, peel and cut in slices. Cook as rapidly as possible. Season with a large piece of butter, pepper and salt, and a little sugar. Canned tomatoes can be used the same way. Serve with toast if desired. A little minced onion flavors them nicely. 4h

GOLD DUST FLOUR

Is Equal to the

BEST.

Highest award at the World's Fair.

AD. ON PAGE 78.

Ask your Grocer for Flour made in

THE

PHOENIX MILL,

And see that you get it.

PHOENIX BEST

Is highly recommended by the author of this book.

AD. ON PAGE 60.

INDEX.

	PAGE.
Angels Food	20
Apple Charlotte	59
Apple Snow	57
Balls for Soup	102
Biscuits	11
Blanc Mange	57
Bread	5 to 9
Breakfast and Tea Cakes	10 to 16
Buckwheat Cakes	13
Cake	17 to 30
Candy	36 to 38
Catsups	130
Charlotte Russe	53 and 55
Cheese Sandwiches	99
Cookies	31 to 35
Corn Beef Hash	99
Creams and Custards	53 to 61
Creams and Ices	41 to 51
Crullers	64
Crumpets	16
Custards	53
Doughnuts and Crullers	63 to 64
Dumplings	102
Dutch Cheese	101
Eggs	65 to 69
Egg Sandwiches	99
Fish	77 to 79
Frappie	45
Fritters	73 to 75
Frosting	71 to 72
Gems	13
Gravies	98
Griddle Cakes	13
Hash	99
Hermits	31
How to Be Happy	32
Ices and Creams	41
Johnny Cake	12
Jumbles	31 and 33
Lettuce Sandwiches	99
Lobsters	102

	PAGE.
Macaroni and Cheese	152
Meats	85 to 93
Meat Pie	101
Mince Meat	107
Miscellaneous Recipes	99 to 102
Muffins	11
Mush	14
Orange Souffle	59
Oyster Dressing	102
Pastry	103 to 110
Peach Cobbler	109
Pickles	111 to 114
Pies	103
Pop Overs	14
Poultry and Game	93 to 97
Preserves and Jellies	115 to 119
Puddings	120 to 126
Pudding Sauce	126 to 129
punches	51
Rolls	12
Salads	133 to 138
Sally Lunn	12
Sauces and Catsups	130 to 132
Scalloped Mutton	101
Shell Fish	81 to 83
Short Cake	109
Snaps	33
Soups	140 to 148
Succotash	151
Tarts	110
Toasts	15
Turbot	79
Turkish Rice	101
Vegetables	149 to 155
Wafers	35
Waffles	14
Washington Pie	109
Welsh Rarebit	15
Yeast	7

Index to Advertisements.

	PAGE.
Adams Manufacturing Co.	160
Anglo-American Drug Company	84
Beeman Chemical Company	26
Val Blatz Brewing Company	80
Bruceline Company	124
California Fig Syrup Company	50
J. W. Cole & Company	54
Crescent Creamery Company	94
Jos. Dixon Crucible Company	34
Dorsett, the Caterer	100
Emerson Drug Company	52
Fountain Spring Water Company	92
Great Northern Soap Co.	139
Max Gessler	90
Healey & Bigelow	74
Holly Flouring Mills	78–155
Fred T. Hopkins	66
E. W. Hoyt & Company	104
W. J. Hurd	68
Minneapolis Brewing Company	38
The Morgan Drug Company	58
New York Condensed Milk Company	42
J. P. Olds	44
J. C. Paul & Company	48
Penna. Salt Manufacturing Company	40
Phœnix Mill Company	60–156
H. B. Platt	108
Ponds Extract Company	128
Radam's Microbe Killer	56
D. Ransom, Son & Company	76
Geo. A. Scott	86–118
Dr. R. Shiffmann	30, 35, 51, 61, 72, 83, 96, 97, 98, 110
Spencerian Medicine Company	70
Swift & Company	4, 22, 108, 135, 148
Swinburne Printing Company	32
Towle Syrup Company	62, 131, 144
Washburn-Crosby Company	88
J. R. Watkins Medical Company	112
Weinhold Drug Company	18–28

WHEN your chairs break, mend them with

ADAMS' LIQUID GLUE, "THE KIND THAT STICKS."

YOU can fasten that leg in your table with

ADAMS' LIQUID GLUE, "THE KIND THAT STICKS."

MEND your bric-a-brac, etc., etc., with

ADAMS' LIQUID GLUE, "THE KIND THAT STICKS."

ANYTHING can be mended to stay with

ADAMS' LIQUID GLUE, "THE KIND THAT STICKS."

USE every precaution to see that you employ

ADAMS' LIQUID GLUE, "THE KIND THAT STICKS."

EVERY BOTTLE WARRANTED TO GIVE ENTIRE SATISFACTION.

WHEN YOU CLEAN HOUSE,

Do not fail to brighten up your old, dull and lustreless Furniture, Piano, Organ, Sewing Machine, etc., with

ADAMS' FURNITURE POLISH,

ADAMS MANUFACTURING CO.,

MINNEAPOLIS, - - MINNESOTA.

www.ingramcontent.com/pod-product-compliance
Lightning Source LLC
Chambersburg PA
CBHW030304170426
43202CB00009B/871